ABOLITIONISM

ABOLITIONISM

A New Perspective

Gerald Sorin

FOREWORD BY JAMES P. SHENTON

PRAEGER PUBLISHERS
New York

PRAEGER PUBLISHERS
A Division of Holt, Rinehart and Winston
200 Park Avenue, New York, N.Y. 10017

© 1972 by Praeger Publishers, Inc.

Library of Congress Catalog Card Number: 79–143981

ISBN 0-275-57630-2
ISBN 0-275-84140-5 (pbk.)

Printed in the United States of America

789   054   987654

To the men and women who, like the abolitionists before them, are working to eliminate social arrangements and states of mind that prevent human fulfillment

Contents

Foreword

by James P. Shenton

Nothing in history is fixed in its interpretation. The historian is forever re-examining evidence or examining new evidence to develop new understandings of past events. As his awareness of the complexity of the human condition and of its social expression deepens, the historian struggles to incorporate these added dimensions within his discipline.

The process of historical reinterpretation, which adds excitement to the task of being a historian, in some measure is a reflection of the changing needs and interests of new generations. More fundamentally, new interpretations of history reflect the profound forces that operate to bring about social change. For the historian, like any other man, is not immune to the influence of the currents that shape the experience and attitudes of his time.

In the decades since the end of World War II, historians have increasingly employed the tools and techniques of analysis developed by sociologists, political scientists, social psychologists, and anthropologists. Armed with these interdisciplinary methods, they have been better equipped to probe the complex motivations of men. Their ability to analyze the extraordinary variety of mass behavior has been vastly improved by the use of statistical analysis and computers to unravel the meaning of mountains of raw data. It now seems possible to explain not only the behavior of a handful of people but that of whole cities, classes, and even societies.

More important than the changes in methodology are the changes in historians' attitudes and approaches, reflecting the impact of vast social changes. Thus, for example, the black revolution in America and abroad has obliged historians to abandon their traditional preoccupation with governing elites to examine the interaction of whites and blacks on all levels of human experience. Americans have suddenly become aware that a vast segment of their national life, that of nonwhites, has been shrouded in neglect. And, because so much of the nonwhite experience has been that of a downtrodden and oppressed people, historians have had to begin to develop techniques of analysis that will permit an understanding of how the common man functioned. In a world growing smaller, a world in which the masses of mankind aspire to a fuller dignity, historians are faced with the demand that they probe the history of the many rather than the few. To meet this demand, they are beginning to explore not only the history of nonwhites but also that of the neglected female. Similarly, historians are beginning to look into the ways in which ethnic origin has affected American whites—for example, the attitudes and behavior of American labor.

The authors of this series, well aware of these significant changes in the world and in historians' ways of interpreting it, are attempting a twofold task. They seek, first, to synthesize the most recent scholarship on a significant period or theme in American history. Second, they attempt to project contemporary relevance into past experience so as to give the student a fresh perspective on material that may be familiar to him in more conventional presentation. The consistent emphasis on changing interpretations, it is hoped, will stimulate interest in history as a dynamic discipline and will dispel any lingering vestiges of the myth that historians are somehow above the fray, uniquely capable of pure objectivity.

With the new effort to understand the individual in mass society has come a desire to know more about the functioning of the institutions that affect everyman. The family, the school, the system of criminal justice, the institutions of government, to name but a few, are being subjected to deepening scrutiny by historians as well as other social scientists.

In the present volume, Professor Sorin has provided an excellent synthesis of the most recent scholarship on abolitionism.

At a time when the country is undergoing a difficult, often agonizing, reappraisal of its racial relations, he has correctly pointed out that recent difficulties in large measure parallel the earlier abolitionist experience. He has avoided the temptation to draw a happy conclusion, pointing out, instead, that the battle for full racial equality is still to be won. And the past is hardly a promising guide. For whatever the achievement of the abolitionists, they left their task incomplete. They thought that the establishment of civil rights would give the black American the necessary armor to win full equality. Perhaps those few abolitionists who called for a provision to assure economic security to the freedmen understood the dilemma that still faces us. Until all men have equal access to property, some men will remain unfree.

Acknowledgments

First and foremost I wish to thank those diligent historians of abolitionism, past and present, from whom I have learned so much. I wish also to thank Carleton Mabee, James P. Shenton, Eric Foner, and Gladys Topkis, of Praeger, for their critical readings of the manuscript and their valuable suggestions. My colleagues at the State University College at New Paltz, Janice Bennett, Donald Roper, Richard Varbero, Allan Spalt, and David Krikun, read all or part of the manuscript and made valuable suggestions. My mother, Ruth Sorin, did an excellent job of typing, for which I am most appreciative. I am especially grateful to my wife, Myra Sorin, for her patience, her perceptive reading, her ability to ask the right questions, and her fine editorial talent.

ABOLITIONISM

1. Introduction

The abolitionists were agitators who hoped to convince their who
fellow Americans that slavery was morally wrong. They often
disagreed among themselves, over both means and ends, but
they were all dedicated to emancipation and concerned about
the tragic human consequences of slavery, especially the victimization of blacks. Many abolitionists were equally committed
to the goal of changing white America's negative consciousness
about blacks in the hope of ending racial discrimination.

The abolitionists, who never made up more than about 1 per
cent of Northern society, differed markedly from the antislavery
people. Large numbers of Americans in the decades prior to the
Civil War shared at least a passive antipathy to the "peculiar
institution." Many were moved to explicit opposition when it
appeared that slavery was having a deleterious effect on the
quality of American life in general. But unlike the abolitionists,
this antislavery group was activated mostly by the belief that
slavery was detrimental to America's economic growth; that the
South's overreaction to criticisms of slavery threatened to undermine white civil liberties; and that slavery and the "slave power"
generally stood opposed to the values of a growing bourgeois
democracy. Most antislavery men and women, at least until the
Civil War, were satisfied merely to advocate containment of
the institution within its existing boundaries. And even when
antislavery people came to see the injustice of slavery itself and
to favor emancipation, they remained uninterested in, and
indeed often violently against, racial integration.

The factors that moved men and women to join the more

radical abolitionist movement are difficult to identify. The evidence is mostly fragmentary, and human motivation is always elusive. Exposure to the values of religious benevolence and evangelism appears to have been important; but since a great many other Americans so exposed did not become abolitionists, a religious explanation alone seems inadequate. Apparently only those predisposed to certain humanitarian values by their family, education, or earlier experiences were so strongly affected by religious revivalism as to embrace abolitionism. It is possible, too, that for many men abolitionism developed out of restrictive, paternalistic concerns and fears. Historian Bertram Wyatt-Brown (1971) has shown that many future abolitionists in the 1820's were critics of secular partisan politics, which they believed competed with the church and irresponsibly seduced and manipulated voters. They were appalled by empty political bombast, which ignored what they considered to be important problems—violations of the Sabbath, dueling, swearing, drunkenness, and vagrancy. They knew that something was wrong in the nation's moral life, and they attempted to make the government and the people of the United States concern themselves with more than matters of self-interest. In the process, they apparently came to see slavery and race prejudice as the source of the nation's spiritual sickness. Religious prohibitions became secondary to a grander vision of a revitalized America—a nation in which no man owned another or discriminated against him on the basis of color.

Whatever their original motivation, when nascent abolitionists first acted on their developing commitment they elicited a severely hostile reaction from white America. As a result, abolitionists asked more searching questions about the nature of a society that espoused freedom and equality, yet defended the oppression, coercion, and gross inequality of slavery and racial discrimination. Many abolitionists, especially the followers of William Lloyd Garrison, were soon persuaded that black slavery was but the most extreme manifestation of what was wrong with America. They discovered other forms of coercion, authoritarianism, and inhumanity in almost all areas of human activity. When mobs, led or manipulated by influential men, denied

basic freedoms to the abolitionists, and when abolitionist ministers were forced out of their churches, many abolitionists began
to realize that their activities were threatening the privilege and
position of established power centers. Gradually they also came
to perceive, especially as they were victimized by it, the central-
ity of violence to much of American life. As this understanding
deepened, they recognized that nothing short of a restructuring
of American society would uproot slavery and racial injustice. It
is this recognition that justifies calling many of the abolitionists
radicals.

There were vital limits to their radicalism. The abolitionist
cause never completely lost its association with paternalism.
Moreover, most abolitionists held middle-class economic values,
and they only partially understood the dynamics and coercive
techniques of class divisions. Yet, they were radical agitators
who recognized that it was necessary to raise the consciousness
of large numbers of people in order to effect a significant social
transformation—a transformation that would include the destruction of an institution that was the base of power of the ruling
class in the South and an important underpinning to the power
of sizable classes in the North. They attempted, in order to
secure racial justice, to eliminate a deeply entrenched racism
and to lay the foundations of a society based on human relationships that transcended the "cash nexus"—a society structured so
as to allow men to fulfill their spiritual and moral potentialities.
This vision ultimately provided whatever moral legitimacy and
revolutionary significance the American Civil War possessed.

The civil rights and black liberation movements of the 1960's
made it clear that many of the problems that had concerned the
abolitionists were still with us. The moral power of the modern
crusade for black freedom forced some historians to take a fresh
look at the abolitionist movement. The result was a sympathetic
although by no means wholly laudatory re-evaluation of the first
militant crusade against racial injustice in America.

The following chapters attempt to deal with many of the questions modern historians have raised about the abolitionist movement. Our position is that, despite their defects of vision and
thought, the abolitionists' activity, as historian Merton Dillon

wrote (1969), "resulted from intense individual commitment to a noble cause." On that account alone their experience might be worthy of study. But more important, the abolitionists made an immeasurable contribution to the tradition of radical reform in America.

2. The Roots of Abolitionism in America

To live in ease and plenty by the toil of those whom violence and cruelty have put in our power, is neither consistent with Christianity nor common justice, and we have good reason to believe draws down the displeasure of Heaven. —Quaker Epistle, 1754

It would be useless for us to denounce the servitude to which the Parliament of Great Britain *wishes to reduce us, while we continue to keep our fellow creatures in slavery just because their color is different from ours.*—BENJAMIN RUSH, 1769

OPenning

Although slavery had existed for centuries without creating overwhelming moral problems for Western man, the institution always seemed inconsistent with his ideals. Thus, wherever slavery existed in Western society, elaborate social and philosophical rationalizations developed. And when the institution, in one of its most oppressive forms, was becoming firmly established in eighteenth-century British America—a place some men had seen as a crucible for human perfection—new tensions were created, which required further restatement and the extension of older Western justifications of slavery. The proslavery defense was not so coherent or unified a body of thought as it was to become in the 1830's, when slavery came under increasing attack. Yet the institution created enough uneasiness to elicit at least erratic, random defenses.

One of the earliest and strongest defenses of American slavery was that it was economically essential. It was possible to contend, given the lack of an alternative labor supply, that European nations could not have settled America and exploited its resources without the aid of African slaves. Indeed, slavery was the basic system of labor in many of the colonies most valued by Europe. And the system was originally defended as of equal benefit to New England fishermen, Pennsylvania farmers, Virginian and Jamaican planters, and British manufacturers.

In colonies not well suited to plantation agriculture, the economy was often based on supplying slave colonies with goods and provisions. Rhode Island and Massachusetts, for example, built ships for the slave trade; the Middle Atlantic colonies sent fish, oats, flour, corn, lumber, hogs, and horses to the planters in the West Indies.

By the late eighteenth century, many wealthy English merchants were engaged in trade with slave colonies, and British manufacturers, refiners, cutlers, coopers, and sailmakers, among others, felt strongly enough involved to petition Parliament at various times in favor of the slave trade. Capital accumulated through investment in slavery and its products helped to finance the construction of English factories and railroads in the eighteenth and nineteenth centuries. And slave-grown cotton, America's principal export and most important cash crop, was the chief raw material for the Industrial Revolution.

Thus men on both sides of the Atlantic who shared the eighteenth century's belief in utility and material progress saw slavery as economically necessary or, as it was sometimes described, as part of the "natural economy of forces."

Still, slavery throughout Western history had been seen by many as the ultimate dehumanization, while the New World represented the promised land where mankind could make a fresh start. In America, far from the decaying vestiges of former tyrannies, where there were no limits to virtue or vice, one might see whether mankind could truly undergo a rebirth and a fulfillment of human aspirations. In the development of American slavery, then, there were profound contradictions that made the institution a source of extraordinary psychic unease. The justification of slavery from the perspective of pure economic utility was insufficient to relieve moral doubt completely.

American slaveholders took some comfort in the thought that they had simply obtained their slaves by purchase from others or by inheritance and bore no moral responsibility for what might have happened in Africa or on the high seas. And Africa was depicted as so despotic and depraved that blacks were said to have little to lose and much to gain by being shipped to America.

Blacks, it was argued, were not only better off out of Africa; they were better off slave than free. The clergyman Cotton Mather told blacks in Massachusetts that they should give up their "fondness for freedom" and recognize that as slaves they lived better than they would as freemen. And British writers claimed that black slaves, whose needs were met from birth to death by their masters, were better off than the wretchedly insecure English lower classes.

These expressions reflected an important assumption that underlay slavery: that some men *by nature* were incapable of maintaining or governing themselves. As historian Winthrop Jordan has shown, when white men first made contact with blacks in Africa, they were already culturally preconditioned to see blackness as something negative or inferior. And African heathenism and open sexuality heightened the impression of the blacks' differences from white Europeans.

When the need to see blacks as an inferior breed of men arose in connection with the defense of slavery, African differences were exaggerated and, despite evidence to the contrary, were taken as proof of racial inferiority. It was argued that blacks were the product of a separate creation, that they bore in their color the mark of ancient sins, and that they were punished with the need for subordination to higher authority. All men, because of their generally debased nature, were so burdened, but blacks more so. This was a return to the ancient argument that slavery was instituted by God for the better ordering of a sinful world. But now the institution served not only as a reminder of the white man's imperfection and a model of his dependence on higher authority; it also kept black sinfulness in check.

Despite these rationalizations, slavery continued to be a source of discomfort even for men whose interests were closely tied to the institution. Throughout the eighteenth century, the problem was intensified by new developments in European and American thought. For it was difficult to escape altogether the feeling that slavery was incompatible with the progress of the scientific enlightenment, the new directions of Christianity, and the developing idea of natural rights.

Enlightenment rationalism, which took root and flourished in eighteenth-century Europe and America, was increasingly used to criticize slavery. Through rational, empirical examination of social relationships, the philosopher Montesquieu, for example, demonstrated that slavery destroyed the humanity of both slave and master and thus violated natural law. The Enlightenment also provided ammunition to critics of slavery in its emphasis on economic mobility and on individual effort and responsibility. But rationalism was also used to defend slavery, for it stressed the slow evolution of institutions and the notion that "Whatever is, is right." Proslavery men could cite the Enlightenment's support of private property and could find in John Locke a "natural" explanation of hereditary inequality. The ideas of the Enlightenment, because they could cut both ways, had a limited effect in creating the state of mind and readiness for action that we call abolitionism. But they did supply the movement with a significant philosophic foundation.

The Enlightenment had great impact, too, on organized religion, and this in turn contributed to the growth of a milieu less tolerant of slavery. The rationalism of the Enlightenment, the implications of modern science, the exciting belief in man's capacity for progressive improvement, and the expanded concern for the life of this world presented a significant challenge to Christianity. To prevent Christian influence from being undermined, sectarian religion would have to be transformed into a more benevolent, worldly creed, with human happiness as at least one of its goals. In Europe, especially among the British Protestants, many sects were indeed moving away from the notion of man as totally corrupt, of misery and subordination as essential parts of life, and of true freedom as unattainable in this world. In short, the concept of original sin was being virtually discarded as a theological foundation, and human nature and conduct were increasingly used as a basis for faith.

These changes amounted to a major religious upheaval and provided Protestantism with a new ethic of benevolence. Benevolence did not lead to abolitionism, however. It led to a doubling of missionary efforts to convert black slaves to a Christian obedience that would enable masters to rule by love instead of force. Christians were not fully to perceive the moral contradictions of slavery until a religious revolution had transformed their ideas of spiritual freedom.

For Americans this transformation began in New England in the 1740's with the significant religious revival known as the Great Awakening. At the core of revivalism was the recognition that sin was not a function of man's predetermined depravity but a worldly fact—that men were free to make choices, and that they were personally responsible for their faith and their actions, or their lack of either. At the same time there was a recognition that no human failings warranted perpetual suffering.

Religious revivalism re-emphasized the spiritual equality implicit in the Christian belief that God, no respecter of worldly status, might give His blessings to the lowliest servant. The Great Awakening was inclusive; it would gather in all the lost sheep; even blacks, even slaves, who found Christ in their hearts could be saved. God's dominant characteristic was increasingly seen to be benevolence, and human happiness His ultimate concern.

Still, none of this led automatically to pleas for emancipation. Eighteenth-century revivalism, in America as in Europe, produced the missionary, not the abolitionist. Americans could not condemn slavery without undermining accepted rationalizations and without questioning the integrity of many of the leaders of the society.

But with the discarding of original sin and with human happiness established as a legitimate religious end, the ancient Christian ideals of liberty, equality, and brotherhood could become powerful weapons in the future struggle to abolish slavery.

Long before the Great Awakening of the 1740's some Christians had begun to see the moral contradiction of American slavery. In the late seventeenth century, Quakers were developing a frame of mind that allowed men to disregard law and precedent and to make judgments by the "Inner Light." By the late eighteenth century the Quakers had played a central role in the abolition of slavery in the North.

Quakers believed in the absolute universality of God's love and therefore in the brotherhood of man. From this perspective, slavery was incompatible with Christian liberty. And for Quakers, with their pacifist principles, slavery presented an additional difficulty; if the slaves should fight for their freedom, could the Quakers condone war against them?

Yet many of the early Quakers were slaveholders. They dealt with the conflict between slaveholding and their religious beliefs by recourse to the ancient dualism of body and soul. However, there is much evidence to suggest that this rationalization, because of Quaker belief and experience, was more difficult for Quakers than for Catholics, Anglicans, or Congregationalists. Men who had suffered religious persecution, as the Quakers had done, were more likely than others to see a connection between physical and spiritual liberty. And thus, although the official Quaker position on slavery changed very slowly, individuals and groups of early Quakers occasionally urged a forthright abolitionist view.

The English founder of the Quaker society, George Fox, reminded American colonists in 1676 that

Christ died for all, both Turks, Barbarians, Tartarians, and Ethyopians; he died for the Tawnies and for the Blacks, as well as for you that are called whites. . . . It will doubtless be very acceptable to the . . . Lord, [if masters let blacks] . . . go free after a considerable Term of Years, if they have served them faithfully; and when they go, and are made free, *let them not go away empty-handed.*

Several Quakers publicly condemned slavery in the English colonies before 1740. As early as 1688, a group of Quakers in Germantown, Pennsylvania, maintained that enslavement was not a question of fate and that purchasing slaves was tantamount to dealing in stolen property. George Keith, who later became the leader of a separatist sect of radical Quakers, emphasized through the 1690's that Christ had died not only to save souls but also to deliver the oppressed, to bring "liberty both inward and outward." And in 1696, at the Quaker Yearly Meeting in Philadelphia, Friends were cautioned by several leaders against trading in blacks as a business or being involved in their further importation. Three decades later, the Yearly Meeting resolved to advise its membership not to purchase slaves even for private use. The Quaker Benjamin Lay made abolitionism the very center of his existence. In the 1730's he spoke out, fasted, and once splattered delegates at a Quaker meeting with the blood of an animal in the hope of awakening their consciences. In order to dramatize the moral urgency of the slavery question, Lay was ready to be ostracized and even to die.

While the specific demands of the most outspoken rebels, like Lay and Keith, were generally ignored, the disturbing questions had been raised, and by the middle of the eighteenth century Quakerism provided a milieu in which hostility to slavery could be something more than individual dissent.

The Quakers' success in awakening others to abolitionism depended on their ability to make men feel personal responsibility for the evils of slavery. John Woolman, a self-effacing Quaker shopkeeper and notary, traveled throughout the Southern colonies in the late 1740's trying to convince other Friends that slaveholding was un-Christian. He often succeeded because he had the ability to see black slavery as something more than an abstract institution; he was convinced that he shared with all America a profound guilt for countenancing it. After hearing Woolman explain why, for example, he could not notarize wills that bequeathed human property, many owners manumitted their slaves.

Woolman emphasized the common denominator—"All Nations

are of one Blood. . . . God's love is universal"—and thus struck squarely at the root of slavery.

> Placing on Men the ignominious Title, SLAVE, dressing them in uncomely Garments, keeping them to Servile Labour, in which they are often dirty, tends gradually to fix a Notion in the Mind, that they are a Sort of People below us in Nature, and leads us to consider them as such in all our Conclusions about them.

He saw the dynamic by which slavery created or reinforced prejudices. In addition to recognizing the crushing effects on the enslaved, Woolman realized that oppression was a two-way street, affecting master as well as slave. "For while the Life of one is made grievous by the Rigour of another, it entails Misery on both."

By the 1740's there was little evidence that the Friends were moving *en masse* to embrace abolition, but the disturbing questions of the past had in some measure prepared them for the crisis they were to face in the 1750's. When large numbers of pacifist Quakers resigned from the Pennsylvania legislature in 1755 because they could not bring themselves to vote appropriations or pay taxes to support the frontier war against the French and Indians, the Friends endured the unpleasant experience of being branded traitors and fanatics by non-Quakers. John Woolman and Anthony Benezet, another great Quaker leader and abolitionist, interpreted the painful situation as deserved punishment for the Quakers' long participation in the sin of slavery. Persecution deepened the Quakers' yearning for withdrawal from evil and their sense of obligation to other victims of hatred and persecution.

Thus black slavery became a symbol of the Quakers' own spiritual bondage, blocking their way to redemption. Manumission of blacks became linked with the Quaker hope for universal emancipation. Finally, at the 1757 Yearly Meeting in Philadelphia, it was resolved that all members who bought or sold blacks were to be excluded from business meetings and from making financial contributions to the Society. In 1773 New England Quakers began to disown members who refused to comply with

antislavery strictures. Ten years later, they initiated a policy
of compensating their former slaves for past services.

New York Quakers moved more slowly at first. In 1762, they
were discouraging the purchase and importation of slaves, as
their coreligionists in Philadelphia had done thirty years earlier.
By 1775 the New York group had disowned slaveholders. Twelve
years later, no slaveholding members were left in any of the
Quaker Societies north of Virginia. Northern Quakers were the
only major religious sect to refuse to hold slaves on grounds of
conscience. And as they were reaching this position, they sought
to convince others as well.

As early as 1767, Anthony Benezet asked the Society for the
Propagation of the Gospel, a missionary enterprise of the Church
of England, to condemn the slave trade. The society responded
that if "the doctrine of the unlawfulness of Slavery should be
taught in our Colonies, . . . Masters . . . will grow more suspicious
and cruel, and much more unwilling to let their Slaves learn
Christianity." What made this answer so frustrating was that
many masters were already unwilling to welcome blacks into
their religious fold, perhaps because, as Winthrop Jordan suggests, the religious conversion "procedure was so thorough and so
patently adaptive that anyone who went through it could
scarcely be denied the status and privileges of full membership." As it was, in the Southern colonies, great numbers of
slaves, possibly a majority, remained outside Christianity.

Benezet found a more responsive audience when he directly
advocated the abolition of slavery. While before 1770 antislavery agitation had failed to induce a single colony to alter its
laws, the response changed radically as the Revolution ap-
proached. For Americans, the imminent conflict gave ideological
force to the libertarian ideas of Montesquieu and other Enlightenment theorists and to the egalitarian doctrines of natural law,
which were embedded in eighteenth-century Western literature.
As the Revolutionary logic unfolded, and as Americans talked
increasingly about the natural rights of man, they moved steadily
toward an environmentalist approach to the cultural differences
among men. For if men universally possessed the same rights
and were in this sense truly created equal, distinctions, were the

product not of the Creator's whim or will but of the environment, or, more appropriately, of "accidental causes." Environmentalism was probably essential to any abolitionist movement; for example, it helped Dr. Benjamin Rush, Revolutionary patriot, to explain away the seeming brutishness of the enslaved black and the supposed "barbarous condition of unenslaved Negroes in Africa."

Moreover, the Revolutionary generation was not simply improvising an ideology to rationalize its desire for independence. It was articulating a system of values emphasizing equality and self-determination, values that were rooted in the seventeenth-century British revolutions and in America's early history, and that now appeared to be threatened by the actions of George III's government. Sincere in their espousal of the rights of man, and convinced that Britain threatened ancient liberties, the leaders of the Revolution increasingly acknowledged that slavery, too, was a violation of natural rights.

Between 1770 and 1810, strong statements against slavery were made by numerous leaders, including John Adams, Benjamin Franklin, Albert Gallatin, Alexander Hamilton, Patrick Henry, John Jay, Thomas Jefferson, James Madison, James Monroe, Harrison Gray Otis, Thomas Paine, and George Washington. John Dickinson published an essay arraying in opposite columns "the speeches and resolutions of the members of Congress in behalf of their own liberty, with their conduct concerning the slavery of others." Abigail Adams put it simply:

It allways appeared a most iniquitous Scheme to me—to fight ourselfes for what we are daily robbing and plundering from those who have as good a right to freedom as we have.

Abolitionists used the opportunity of the Revolution to charge that advocates of independence who were not also committed to antislavery were trifling patriots who made a mockery of the liberties of mankind. For as John Allen, a New Hampshire abolitionist, wrote accusingly:

. . . while you are fasting, praying, nonimporting, nonexporting, remonstrating, resolving and pleading for a restoration of your charter rights, you at the same time are continuing this lawless, cruel, inhuman, and abominable practice of enslaving your fellow creatures.

This kind of attack on slavery was so pervasive that black slaves, in the North at least, saw no danger in adding their voices to the denunciation of the institution. In 1776 a group of Massachusetts blacks petitioned the government for their freedom, saying that they expected "great things from men who have made such a noble stand against the designs of their *fellow-men* to enslave them." In 1777, drawing an analogy between their case and the claims of the patriots, they wrote: "Every principle from which America has acted in the course of her difficulties with Great-Britain, pleads stronger than a thousand arguments for your Petitioners."

George Washington's statement in 1774 that "we must assert our rights . . . [or become] tame and abject slaves, as the blacks we rule over with such arbitrary sway," underscored the contradiction between black slavery and the patriot cause. Quakers and other religious leaders attempted with some success to exploit the contradiction by using the Declaration of Independence and the Revolution to advance among the populace the convictions about equality that they had already reached on religious and moral grounds. Samuel Hopkins, a New England minister whom Jonathan Edwards had converted to religious evangelism during the Great Awakening, used the context of the Revolution to argue that "by the immutable laws of Nature, all men are entitled to life and liberty." Hopkins had long before interpreted Edwards' idea of "benevolent, disinterested affection" to mean that God commands mankind to benevolence toward those who need it most, and had preached that slavery was simply contrary to God's will.

Revivalists used another, older religious notion to convince Americans of their guilt in slaveholding. America was said to be a covenanted community—inhabited by God's chosen people. More was expected of man here than elsewhere. That the community was suffering now was punishment for its past sins.

British encroachments, then, were indications of America's guilt. For however free and virtuous individuals might be, the sins of the community or the nation would be repaid in kind by all. Taxes and commercial restraint could be seen as punishment for the sins of greed and luxury. And the threat of political bondage revealed the source of the colonists' most profound guilt—enslavement of their fellow men. By placing the contradiction between the American libertarian ideology and practice toward blacks in the framework of a long-familiar religious formula of sin and punishment, abolitionists enormously enhanced the anti-slavery appeal.

Moreover, in the context of the Revolution, it was very difficult for American ministers of any denomination to urge black slaves who had become Christians to remain content in their bondage while they were encouraging white members of their congregations to resist royal oppression. The ministers were immersed in an intellectual current that was carrying them and so many others toward new moral beliefs.

The new religious, humanitarian, and environmental ideas had linked freedom for blacks and the coming of the Revolution. And the ideology of the Revolution further advanced the possibility of freedom for blacks. The statement of a conference of Virginia Methodists demonstrates how intimately the strands of thought were interconnected:

> We view as contrary to the Golden Law of God on which hang all the Law and the Prophets and the Unalienable Rights of Mankind, as well as every Principle of the Revolution, to hold in deepest Debasement, in a more abject slavery than is perhaps to be found in Any part of the World except America, so many souls that are capable of the image of God.

Another important factor linking black freedom to the Revolution was the manpower demands of the war itself. Manpower problems between 1777 and 1779 made Rhode Island, Connecticut, and New York more attentive to abolitionist pleas; all three states passed bills either granting unconditional manumission to slaves who enlisted in the army or making it easier for masters to manumit slaves who could then join the war effort. And black performance in the conflict made it more difficult to deny the black's manhood and right to freedom.

Although many religious groups, including Baptists, Congregationalists, Methodists, and Presbyterians, now shared antislavery attitudes, most of the real work of emancipation was done by the Quakers. Anthony Benezet badgered the delegates to the Continental Congress in 1774 until they agreed to call for a cessation of slave imports and a boycott of merchants who refused to cooperate. And the first secular abolitionist organization, the Society for the Relief of Free Negroes Held in Bondage, formed in 1775, was organized mainly by Philadelphia Quakers.

Between 1777 and 1804, all states from Pennsylvania north provided effectively for the eventual abolition of slavery; in fact, all but two, New York and New Jersey, had done so by 1784. This accomplishment reflected the spread of the Revolutionary egalitarian ideology as well as increasing antislavery agitation by Quakers and, to a lesser extent, Methodists, Congregationalists, and Baptists. The Quaker plea that slavery was incompatible with Christian ideals had prepared the way for the Revolutionary argument that it was irreconcilable with the rights of man. While Quakers had been unable to defeat slavery armed only with moral arguments, the philosophy of the Revolution allowed them to portray slavery as a gross contradiction of American political values. Only then did they meet with some success.

In any case, abolition of slavery in the North was no small feat. Historian Arthur Zilversmit, in the *First Emancipation* (1967), has clearly demonstrated that, although the slave population of the North was relatively small, black slavery was a common and accepted practice. Indeed, in parts of the North, the plantation system was reproduced on a small scale, as were some of slavery's more rigorous safeguards, including "black codes" in New York and New Jersey which imposed stringent restrictions on all blacks, free and slave. And while slavery as an economic institution was not central to Northern development, it was profitable for individual slaveholders, who strenuously resisted both general abolition and individual suits for freedom. A great many Northerners, acutely conscious of the rights of property (also emphasized in the Revolutionary ideology), supported the masters in their attempts to hold onto their chattels.

Quaker and Revolutionary agitation did help to win gradual emancipation for blacks in Pennsylvania, Rhode Island, New York, and New Jersey, and succeeded in persuading the Massachusetts courts to interpret the new state constitution as an antislavery document; but the principal concern of Northern white society reflected in these decisions was the immediate welfare of whites rather than the future benefit of manumitted slaves. Masters, in some cases, were compensated or were relieved of any responsibility for their former slaves' sustenance. At the same time, little or nothing was done to erase the debilitating effects of slavery on the freed blacks.

It was therefore necessary for Quakers throughout the Northern states to dedicate themselves to aims beyond emancipation, including work through the Society for the Relief of Free Negroes, and the Society for Improving the Condition of the Colored Race. In New York and Pennsylvania, these abolitionist societies devoted their efforts to implementing existing laws to protect blacks. Of what use to the black man, Quakers asked, was manumission alone? He must have "civil privileges," and society must prepare him to exercise them. Despite their intensity and sincerity, Quakers achieved only partial success. For while the Northern population could be converted to antislavery—that is, convinced that slavery was wrong—it had still to be converted to abolitionism—i.e., the belief that political and economic equality for blacks, although not necessarily social equality, was right.

With the passage of a gradual abolition law by New Jersey in 1804, the idea that slavery must be put on the road to extinction had triumphed throughout the North. The Quaker abolitionists now turned more of their attention to the South.

The South experienced many of the same forces of humanitarianism, evangelism, and natural rights philosophy that helped to create an atmosphere conducive to antislavery in the North. But here, especially as Revolutionary sentiment waned, a whole society continued to accommodate itself physically and emotionally to a system of slavery that was not only pervasive but apparently, as historian Robert McColley has demonstrated (1964), increasingly successful as a social and economic institution.

During the Revolutionary period, criticism of slavery was relatively widespread and accepted in Virginia, Maryland, and Delaware. Jefferson and Madison introduced measures to soften the Virginia law against manumission, and they hesitantly and unsuccessfully made recommendations of eventual emancipation. The number of manumissions in Maryland and Virginia in the 1780's and early 1790's has been described as a veritable flood. Virginia's free black population actually doubled between 1782 (when the liberalized manumission law was passed) and 1784. Laws were passed in other Southern states facilitating private manumissions. These states conceded a certain legitimacy to independent antislavery sentiment but resisted sweeping political action. As far south as Georgia, new laws made gross maltreatment of slaves illegal. Even if these were not enforced, a subtle though important change of mind had apparently been effected.

While some Southerners remained untouched by Revolutionary libertarianism or failed to see its connection to slavery, many others revealed a feeling of tension over their opposition to slavery in principle and their accommodation to the system for its advantages in practice. This would never lead, however, to any serious attempt to end the institution.

In the upper South, there were significant numbers of Quakers and Methodists and some Presbyterians who believed that slavery was inconsistent with the Christian ethic and who were fundamentally committed to gradual abolition of the institution. But there were no antislavery organizations south of Virginia (except Friends in North Carolina).

Everywhere in the South, many thoughtful masters seem to have had cautious hopes of ameliorating the worst evils of slavery so that the black slave would give his services without coercion. Such hopes were spoiled by the simple fact, obscured for years in America by the rhetoric of racism, law, philosophy, and even religion, that a slave was not simply a piece of property but a man held down by force. After 1790, as the Revolution receded and the fear of black rebellion increased, in part as a result of a bloody slave revolt in Santo Domingo, antislavery sentiment, while not dead, no longer grew in the South. By the turn of the century, private manumissions had become more difficult even in the upper South. The economic advantages of slavery were more evident, and the racial prejudices of white Americans not only created immense fear of the free black but made it easier to justify slavery. Jefferson was sometimes ambivalent about it but he, too, thought blacks were an inferior breed of men. And while in private letters he continued to advocate emancipation and resettlement of blacks, he actually thought a massive operation of this sort was nearly impossible. Thus the proposed Ordinance of 1784, restricting slavery in the Northwest Territories, marked Jefferson's last public attempt to limit or end the institution. By 1805 Jefferson said, "I have long since given up the expectation of any early provision for the extinguishment of slavery among us."

In the eighteenth century the foundations of the abolitionist movement were laid by an intellectual revolution that was affecting the entire Western world. In America, where mankind appeared to have a chance to make a fresh start, unfettered by the errors of the past—e.g., authoritarianism and stratification— the implications of the new secular consciousness of the Enlightenment were especially intense. The great religious reawakening of the 1740's reinforced the concept of Christian egalitarianism, which, in its new context, could mean physical as well as spiritual freedom. Finally, the Revolutionary philosophy of natural rights, developing at about the same time, created an intellectual climate within which it was difficult to deny the black's claim to freedom.

Abolitionists exploited this atmosphere in attempting to end human enslavement in the North and to gain some amelioration for black slaves, even if only in the statute books, in the South. Yet the eighteenth- and early nineteenth-century movement essentially failed. Not only did the overwhelming majority of Southern blacks remain slaves, but emancipated blacks North and South continued to face devastating obstacles to real freedom. The natural rights philosophy showed its limits here, for it emphasized property rights, which hindered emancipation efforts; more importantly, by viewing society as cemented mainly by legal relations, the natural rights philosophy directed attention to the black's technical status instead of to his actual condition. Quakers and members of other religious groups that viewed society as held together by moral relations made the critical affirmation that outward legal status was not all that mattered. But some of them, too, had no love for the black man. Moreover, they did not have a popular following. Despite the moderate aims, restrained conduct, and conservative membership of the various abolitionist societies, they frequently aroused hostility on both sides of the Mason-Dixon line.

The great limiting factor for abolitionist growth was racism—a racism that knew no sectional or ideological boundaries. A belief in the inferiority of the black pervaded the consciousness of white America; abolitionists themselves did not escape it entirely. This belief, whether or not it was culturally ingrained in whites prior to the enslavement of blacks, was certainly heightened by slavery, which degraded and brutalized its victims. Furthermore, as slavery became more entrenched and its social and economic advantages more apparent, white men found it harder to give up. Faced with the continued existence of an "evil" institution in a "good" society, defenders of slavery articulated and internalized a more thoroughly racist rationale for the institution.

Encouraged, then, to some extent by Christian egalitarianism, by the philosophy of natural rights, and by the rhetoric of the Revolution, the growth of abolitionism in early America was concomitantly limited by concepts of property rights and by racism. The movement had developed in fits and starts. It had achieved some partial successes (e.g., the abolition of slavery in the North), but by 1810 it seemed moribund. Two decades later abolitionism was resurrected in more intense form by men and women inspired more by Christian egalitarianism than by natural rights: men and women who, to a remarkable degree (though by no means completely), transcended racial prejudice, and who would attempt to convince their countrymen to do the same.

3. The Rise of Immediatism

*Urge immediate abolition as earnestly as we may, it will alas! be
gradual abolition in the end. We have never said that slavery would be
overthrown by a single blow; that it ought to be we shall always
contend.* —WILLIAM LLOYD GARRISON, 1831

The doctrine of immediatism, which became pervasive in abolitionist ranks in the 1830's, was misinterpreted by much of the
American public to mean instant and unconditional freeing of
the slaves—a course of action that most abolitionists actually
thought would be madness. As far as abolitionists were concerned, immediatism described a state of mind: recognition of
the sinfulness of slavery, admission of personal responsibility for
its existence, and personal commitment to make no compromise
with it. Immediatism also described a program of direct action
designed to achieve total emancipation in the future. The New
England Anti-Slavery Society issued the following definition in
1833:

> What, then, is meant by IMMEDIATE ABOLITION? . . .
> It means . . . that every [black] husband shall have his own wife,
> and every wife her own husband, . . . united in wedlock . . ., and
> placed under the protection of law. . . .

It means that [black] parents shall have the control and government of their own children, and that the children shall belong to their parents. . . .

It means . . . that the . . . power . . . to punish . . . slaves without trial . . . shall be at once taken away. . . .

It means . . . providing schools and instruction [for slaves]. . . .

It means . . . right . . . over wrong, . . . love over hatred, and religion over heathenism.

A letter in the Boston *Recorder and Telegraph* (1825) signed Vigornius put it simply: *"The slave-holding system must be abolished:* and in order to the accomplishment of this end, *immediate,* determined measures must be adopted for the *ultimate* emancipation of every slave."

Immediatism, in addition, was a simple tactical approach. Immediatists agreed with Elizur Wright, Secretary of the American Anti-Slavery Society (founded in 1833), that "all the gradual reformation in practice, which has blessed the world, has been the fruit of stern immediatism in doctrine." Thus militant abolitionists asked that Americans, North and South, adopt a moral disposition to see slavery as an unmitigated evil and to feel a "present" or "immediate obligation" to do something about ending it eventually.

Gradualism, which was the dominant state of mind among abolitionists in the late eighteenth and early nineteenth centuries, had also looked forward to eventual emancipation. But it assumed that progress was practically inevitable, and the abolitionists' confidence on this point smothered any sense of moral urgency.

Gradualism, moreover, was reinforced by profound anxiety over the future of the emancipated slave. Colonization—i.e., the deportation of freed blacks—became an important part of the gradualist program, especially in the South. In the early nineteenth century the majority of abolitionists in the North, where the black population was small and emancipation presented no massive problem of police control or economic dislocation, were not especially attracted to proposals for black removal. But Northern abolitionists, most of whom had initially accepted a gradualist approach, did not denounce colonization or rule it out as a practicable solution to the slavery problem.

Many of the men who maintained that the colonization of blacks in the American West, the Caribbean, or Africa was essential to an effective antislavery movement were not truly abolitionists by our definition, for they believed with Jefferson that "blacks ... are inferior to the whites in the endowments both of body and mind" and that "the two races, equally free, cannot live in the same government" without destroying the society. And since wholesale emancipation appeared to threaten wholesale intermixture, many Southern antislavery men regarded black removal as indispensable. Indeed, some of the abolitionists, North and South, although not themselves racist, thought removal was necessary to make emancipation feasible in a racist American society. Even some of the most fervent egalitarians espoused black expatriation, for they feared, with an anonymous New Hampshire abolitionist, that, because of white prejudices, "if the negroes should remain among us ... they will not be treated upon terms of equality."

As the nineteenth century advanced, the colonization movement lost much of its antislavery thrust and was paradoxically transformed into a proslavery proposal. Colonization increasingly became an effort to free America from the danger of slave insurrection. The free black was to be removed because he was a threat, a model for rebellious slaves and a potential accomplice of fugitive slaves. During the 1790's, a rebellion of black slaves and mulattos in nearby French Santo Domingo had literally decimated the colony's white population. The rebellion, which grew out of the French Revolution, led to a series of scares and suspected plots in Virginia, South Carolina, and Louisiana. The bloody devastation in the Caribbean was a virtual obsession in Southern states, parts of which were more heavily populated by blacks than whites. The abortive Gabriel uprising, a threatened slave insurrection near Richmond in 1800, gave evidence of significant planning among slaves and was followed by numerous hysterical rumors, from Virginia to Louisiana. This stoked the fear of a widespread rebellion of slaves. And the specter of slave insurrection haunted the South after 1800.

Slave rebellion was also a galling reminder that slaveholding violated the purpose for which the nation was founded. If slaves wanted and were ready to fight for their liberty like other men, the presumption of inequality, a significant proslavery defense, was negated. Men who wished to preserve slavery, then, needed to reduce the possibility of slave rebellion, and the removal of freed blacks was seen as a necessary step in this direction. Understandably, colonization appealed to defenders of slavery, and the movement, while entering a period of relative decline between 1805 and 1816, continued to attract the interest of proslavery as well as antislavery men and abolitionists. When the American Colonization Society was founded, in 1817, its support came mainly from non-abolitionists. In 1821, the president of the Society, Supreme Court Justice Bushrod Washington, of Virginia, sold half his slaves to the deep South. It is hard to imagine any abolitionist or sincere antislavery man so doing. During the 1820's and early 1830's, the Society's leaders included several men who later became militant abolitionists—e.g., Gerrit Smith, Samuel J. May, and Joshua Leavitt—but, nevertheless, colonization by the third decade of the nineteenth century had undergone a general reversal of intention.

Most abolitionists eventually came to see that the effective destruction of slavery depended on the extirpation of racial prejudice. To continue to insist on colonization was, at the least, to imply a difference in the black man that amounted to inferiority. Immediatists therefore rejected colonization as a racist escape on the part of American society generally, as a deception on the part of the gradualists (who, they said, wished to induce gradual indifference to the existence of slavery), and as unconscious hypocrisy on the part of abolitionists.

While the idea of colonizing America's blacks almost disappeared among the new breed of abolitionists, who were vitally concerned about the victimization of blacks, it had staying power within the antislavery movement, which aimed at reducing slavery's negative effects on white society. Colonization proposals re-emerged sporadically in the antebellum period, urged mainly by antislavery men using explicitly racist arguments. Lincoln flirted with the idea as late as 1865. (At times, especially after 1850, some black leaders who feared that white prejudice would never permit black equality also supported colonization.) The persistence of the idea of colonization within the antislavery movement underscored America's development as both a racist and materialist, and a libertarian and egalitarian society. As Jefferson's tortured writings on the subject show, sensitive men were torn by what they saw as the terrible consequences of either maintaining or abolishing slavery.

In the 1830's, however, many abolitionists were generally able to transcend racial prejudice sufficiently to discard gradualism and to commit themselves fearlessly to the destruction of slavery. But this did not mean that immediatists gave up altogether what they considered to be viable gradual plans. Benjamin Lundy, a crusading Baltimore Quaker, worked for publicly supported voluntary colonization plans as late as 1835. At the same time he implored the North to receive the freed black without restriction and pleaded with the South to be nondiscriminating toward its black population. In his newspaper, *The Genius of Universal Emancipation*, Lundy printed many plans for gradual freedom, but, discouraged by lack of support in the North and overreaction in the South, he discontinued the practice in 1825.

Even though the abolitionists were beginning to realize the wisdom of Boston lawyer Wendell Phillips' assertion that "If we would get half a loaf, we must demand the whole of it," many abolitionist writings in the 1820's and 1830's continued to advocate gradual freedom for slaves. Even William Lloyd Garrison, editor of the militant abolitionist newspaper, *The Liberator*, and dean of the immediatists, was willing, as late as 1832, to hold newly freed slaves in "the benevolent restraints of guardianship." However, the abolitionists' most gradual plans to free blacks were seen, especially in the South, as barely disguised proposals for anarchy and miscegenation. It appears, then, that abolitionists were driven toward immediatism in part by the negative reaction to gradualism.

Another important factor in discrediting gradualism was the increasing militancy of blacks, free and slave. Although some blacks supported emigration, large groups of blacks repudiated the colonization movement as not only gradualist but retrogressive. Colonization, a spokesman for the Philadelphia black community proclaimed in 1817, "must insure to the [black] multitudes . . . Misery, *sufferings, and perpetual slavery*." Pittsburgh blacks meeting in 1831 believed that "African colonization is a scheme to drain the better informed part of the colored people out of these United States, so that the chain of slavery may be rivetted more tightly." They considered "every colored man who allows himself to be colonized in Africa, or elsewhere, a traitor to . . . [the] cause." They resolved that they were "just as much natives here as the members of the Colonization Society. . . . Here we were born—here will we live . . . and here we will die."

Black militancy expressed itself in other ways, too. In 1822, in the area surrounding Charleston, South Carolina, where blacks made up more than half the population, a widespread plot to rebel, initiated by freeman Denmark Vesey, was uncovered and suppressed by banishment and execution. Some have argued with historian Richard C. Wade (1964) that the plot "was probably never more than loose talk by aggrieved and embittered men," but the evidence appears to indicate that there was careful planning, organizing, and recruiting for well over a year, and that perhaps upwards of 9,000 black slaves were involved. In 1831, the same year as the Pittsburgh anti-colonization meeting, bloody slave revolts had erupted in Virginia and Jamaica, and two years earlier the radical black abolitionist David Walker had managed to circulate a revolutionary appeal among the slaves in several Southern states. This overt and threatened violence made some abolitionists fearful of losing white support, but it shook many others out of gradualism. It was harder to believe now that slavery would simply progress to a peaceful and final disappearance. Thus the old conviction that slavery was evil stimulated a new sense of moral urgency. If slavery was to be abolished, and without violence, then some form of *intense moral activity*, the abolitionists believed, was necessary.

The Southern response to black militancy was greater repression. In the winter of 1831–32, a convention was held in Virginia to discuss the implications of the recent Nat Turner rebellion in that state. After a debate that touched on many phases of the slavery problem, various proposals for emancipation were defeated, and laws were passed for greater restriction of the black population. The Virginia decision was crucial in a number of ways. Virginia was the state, abolitionists had believed, that would lead the South out of slavery. Virginia had had a history of antislavery sentiment (though no significant action) among its most important leaders; its black population was relatively small (compared to the proportion of blacks to whites in South Carolina, for instance); and slavery was no longer assumed to be economically beneficial to the state. That Virginia did not use the 1831–32 opportunity to abolish slavery or at least put it on the road to gradual extinction convinced many abolitionists that their faith in inevitable progress was ill founded.

The Virginia debates also appear to have influenced other Southern states that were seeking ways to avoid slave uprisings. Immediately after the Virginia convention, beginning in North Carolina and spreading to all the slave states, "black codes" were made more restrictive. Laws were passed curbing the mobility of slaves through a system of patrols and passes, meetings of slaves were prohibited, educational possibilities were curtailed, and the possibility of manumission was reduced. Free blacks were not spared; they, too, had similar disabilities imposed on them. In such a context it is understandable that men committed to the abolition of slavery saw the need for a change in approach to the problem. To some degree, then, immediatism was a creation of the slaveholders themselves.

The acceptance of immediatism in abolitionist ranks was also a product of religious revivalism. Between 1825 and 1832 a "mighty revival," often called the Second Great Awakening, swept many parts of the country, especially the Northeast. Revivalist ministers like Charles Grandison Finney in New York and Lyman Beecher in New England used the evangelical vehicle to carry a socio-theological message to larger and larger audiences. The revivalists believed in a new, more immediate relation between man and God and man and his fellow creatures —one that emphasized perfectibility rather than inability, activity rather than passivity, benevolence rather than piety.

The teachings of the evangelists between 1820 and 1840 were the culmination of religious developments of the preceding century. Orthodox religion had been undermined by secular, rationalistic beliefs. Strict theological doctrines had been increasingly qualified since the middle of the eighteenth century. In northeastern America, the result was a peculiar synthesis of Calvinist and liberal doctrines. Retaining the ideas of sin and imperfect sanctification, religious leaders adopted certain humanistic notions. Thus Finney, Beecher, and others, suspecting that the natural tendency of men was toward degeneracy and sin, nonetheless believed progress to be attainable by human effort, but only through diligence and constant reminder.

Sin, they believed, was the consequence of moral, not natural inability. All men were capable of a perfect conformity to God's law. Only the want of willingness could frustrate this possibility. It was the aim of the religious revivals to develop that willingness and turn it into commitment. Finney assumed that the individual had free will and the moral ability to work out his own salvation. "Unless the will is free," the great evangelist wrote, "man has no freedom; and if he has no freedom, he is not a moral agent." So defined, man's role in the drama of salvation was central and dynamic.

Although the primary concern of revivalists was the salvation of souls, Finney and his co-workers dwelled more upon the specific sins of men in society than on abstract and heated theological appeals and arguments. The emphasis was on good works as much as faith. And audiences were told that benevolence was more than emotion—it was action. The evangelists used their texts to build in their audiences a sense of personal responsibility for slavery, intemperance, and war, and a present obligation to act against such sins.

The aim of Finney and other evangelists was to make salvation the beginning rather than the end of religious experience. The convert would begin a new life in which, Finney said, he "should set out with a determination to aim at being useful in the highest degree possible." Reform activity, then, would not only bring justification to the convert but would help bring the millenium, or salvation, to the world.

The Michigan abolitionist leader Seymour Treadwell wrote to his son:

> If the three millions of our fellow beings remain much longer in bondage and our country thereby shall sink to ruin, it shall not be for the want of my humble efforts to prevent a calamity so direful to the human race—I feel that woe is unto me unless I am found laboring and talking in the cause.

While there was concern for self in their motivation, that concern was intimately tied to what the abolitionists believed were the needs of the slaves and the nation.

At any rate, to the convert fresh from the revival, social ills seemed easily curable. Nineteenth-century reformers tried utopian communities, like Brook Farm and Oneida. They espoused sweeping changes in diet, prison reform, women's rights, temperance, peace, and the abolition of slavery. They believed that in these areas reform could be accomplished quickly and permanently.

Emancipation, then, was the immediate right of the slave, the immediate duty of the master, and the immediate obligation of the Christian citizen. But the actual operation of the doctrine of immediate emancipation, Congregational minister Amos A. Phelps wrote in 1834, "may be gradual on the community." Only one slaveholder at a time might yield to the pressure of immediate duty to free his slave; only one citizen at a time might yield to the pressure of immediate duty to end his complicity with slavery. But this would not prevent the convert from taking an immediatist position; on the contrary, it encouraged him. In order to achieve gradual abolition it would be necessary to "urge immediate abolition as earnestly" as possible. Elizur Wright wrote in 1833, "The firm expression of an enlightened public opinion ... in favor of instant abolition, is ... the only effectual means of securing abolition in any time whatsoever."

Religious evangelism, then, helped to build immediate emancipation in a number of ways. It re-awakened and redirected religious impulses, and it articulated the religious developments and innovations of recent decades that were giving a social connotation to sin and substituting benevolent activity for piety. By emphasizing the possibility of human perfection through choice and at the same time focusing on the sin of slavery, evangelism engendered personal commitment to abolitionism and to an immediate approach to reform. Evangelism also provided the vocabulary and method of the new militant abolitionism. There were doctrinal similarities between immediate repentance and immediate emancipation. And acceptance of immediate emancipation, according to historian David Brion Davis, was the sign "of an immediate transformation within the reformer himself; as such, it was seen as an expression of inner freedom, of moral sincerity and earnestness, and of victory over selfish and calculating expediency."

Unconditional attack, moreover, had been the successful method of the revivalists in the work of conversion, and abolitionist crusaders saw no reason to discard a weapon that had been effective. Furthermore, most of the individual evangelists themselves dispersed into the reform movements, including abolitionism.

Most important of all, evangelism gave fresh meaning to the lives of many Christian men who were troubled by a changing and materialistic world. It was a practical faith which saw sin in worldly, concrete terms—in evil actions and oppressive institutions; it built in its converts a present obligation to fight sin; and it optimistically predicted the abolition of sin as a giant step toward the building of God's kingdom on earth.

Certainly, it appears that the vast majority of abolitionists were religious men and women who were affected by the evangelism of the era. Historian Gilbert Hobbs Barnes estimates that at a typical abolitionist convention, two-thirds of the delegates were ministers. And in Michigan and New York, the only states in which the social bases of abolitionist leadership have been systematically studied, the great majority of abolitionist leaders were active and intense religious evangelists. In New York, 68 per cent of the leaders "had either been ministers, trustees or founders of churches, deacons, elders, missionaries, superintendents of Sunday Schools or active in evangelical societies." Most of the abolitionists were either Presbyterian or Congregational. The religious zeal of these leaders was engendered and reinforced when they were exposed to religious revivals in New England and New York. And many of the abolitionists were directly affected by Finney, who held major revival meetings in New York City and Rochester, or by Theodore Dwight Weld, Finney's foremost convert and collaborator in the work of salvation.

In Michigan, 60 per cent of the abolitionist leaders were pastors, deacons, or elders (again, mainly Presbyterian or Congregational), and approximately 70 per cent spent at least three years of their adult lives in New York or New England between 1824 and 1833, the period of the Great Revival in these areas. After leaving the East, moreover, Michigan abolitionists did not escape exposure to ardent clerical champions of abolitionism. The evangelist John P. Cleaveland, influential pastor of the First Presbyterian Church in Detroit, pitched his sermons in a sociopolitical key, taking his audiences along the road to abolitionism.

 Several key figures in the movement, including William Lloyd Garrison, Theodore Dwight Weld, Lewis Tappan, Henry B. Stanton, and Gerrit Smith, had important religious experiences which influenced their commitment to abolitionism. Ideologically the most uncompromising of the abolitionists, Garrison served the cause mainly as an editor—for a short time in slave-owning Baltimore, where he was jailed for two months for writing against a slave trader—and from 1831 to 1865 in Boston, where he edited the abolitionist paper *The Liberator*. One of Garrison's major contributions, beyond his frequent and consistent example of personal courage, was sorting out complex situations and defining the issues for the abolitionists.

Garrison had been reared as a Baptist with Calvinist inclinations. He moved from religious orthodoxy to religious liberalism during the era of evangelical revivalism, because of the influence of close associates who were liberal Quakers and partly because of the churches' reluctance to oppose slavery.

In 1828, Garrison, then 22 years old, met the zealous Quaker and abolitionist Benjamin Lundy. Lundy was influential in escalating Garrison's commitment to abolitionism and in convincing him that men should accept nothing on authority. Lundy also moved Garrison toward the religious belief that all coercion, including political coercion, was immoral and should be removed from human relationships. Eventually Garrison molded these ideas into a personal philosophy of noncoercion or nonresistance which he, and an important group of followers, advocated in addition to the abolition of slavery and racial integration.

Theodore Dwight Weld, whose powerfully persuasive manner and oratory converted several leading men to immediatism, was the son of a minister. And at his uncle's home near Utica, New York, Theodore frequently met Charles Stuart, a leading pietist and distributor of Bibles and religious tracts. Stuart became Weld's model and source of inspiration.

In the winter of 1825, when Charles Grandison Finney's Great Revival came to Utica, Charles Stuart and Theodore Dwight Weld were converted and joined Finney's "holy band" of assistant revivalists. Stuart went to England in 1829 to join the movement to abolish slavery in the West Indies. He beseiged Weld with letters commending abolitionism, and by 1830 Weld was expressing a militant antislavery sentiment.

In 1833, Weld, then a student at the Lane Theological Seminary, organized a debate on slavery and abolition and, through it, virtually the entire student body was converted to immediatism. Many of the students went on to become abolitionist agents, lecturing and soliciting funds. Weld's main talent was his oratory, and he is credited by contemporaries and historians alike with singlehandedly abolitionizing northeastern Ohio. He was in constant peril from mobs but did not flinch. He stopped his lecture tours only when his voice ran out.

Weld was an agitator. He recognized that it was necessary to shake great numbers of people out of their indifference before important social changes could be effected. Toward this end, he helped to organize the first nationwide petition campaign; he formed an "army" of some seventy antislavery agents to abolitionize the North; and, with the help of his wife, Angelina Grimké, and her sister, Sarah, Weld wrote abolitionism's most famous propaganda tract—*Slavery as It Is*. Weld made another major contribution to the movement by guiding and encouraging antislavery Congressmen in their struggles against proslavery measures in the 1840's and by lobbying in Washington among Congressmen not yet converted to antislavery.

Another central figure in the abolitionist crusade was Lewis Tappan, a wealthy New York silk merchant, who, with his brother Arthur, underwrote many abolitionist activities and institutions. Arthur played a generally passive role in the movement; Lewis Tappan gave enormous amounts of time and energy as well as money. He was representative of many abolitionists who believed in moral suasion but who, frustrated by their countrymen's failure to become abolitionists, eventually broke with Garrison and his followers and resorted to the political system as a means to effect their ends.

The Tappans were brought up in a strictly religious household and, as they began to accumulate wealth in the late 1820's, they also began, as Lewis wrote, "to reflect seriously upon [their] obligations as . . . steward[s] of the lord." When Charles Grandison Finney brought his "Great Revival" to New York City in 1830, the Tappan brothers fell under his influence. Lewis and Arthur founded the *New York Evangelist* to publish Finney's views, including those on slavery, and to spread religious revivalism throughout the nation. Whenever Finney's disciple, abolitionist Theodore Dwight Weld, was in New York, he and Lewis Tappan had long conversations. "It was during these sessions," according to Tappan's biographer, that Lewis "came to understand immediate abolitionism."

Like the Tappans, Gerrit Smith, the owner of a monumental fortune, used his wealth to underwrite scores of abolitionist projects. In the late 1840's, Smith became the gubernatorial and presidential candidate of the abolitionist Liberty party.

Religion appears to have been an important factor in Gerrit Smith's militancy in the crusade against slavery. His father and wife were both devoutly religious and the latter worked hard to convert her husband to evangelism. Between 1825 and 1835 a series of religious revivals occurred around the area of Smith's home in Peterboro, New York. Smith's biographer contends that "long-continued and high-powered evangelistic pressure," applied by the community, by his wife, and by his father, was probably responsible for Smith's "entrance upon the work of regenerating his fellow men."

In any event, Gerrit Smith attended numerous revival meetings in the early 1830's. By 1835 he had opened, in Peterboro, a manual-labor school for blacks; in the same year he withdrew from the gradualist American Colonization Society to join the recently organized New York State Anti-Slavery Society, which worked for immediate emancipation without expatriation and for civil rights for freedmen.

New York lawyer Henry Brewster Stanton, instrumental in moving abolitionism into politics and one of the most effective administrative officers in the crusade against slavery, was another of Charles Grandison Finney's converts. Soon after Stanton was influenced by Finney, he went to study at Lane Theological Seminary, where fellow student Theodore Dwight Weld moved him even further in the direction of abolitionism.

Most abolitionist leaders were influenced by evangelical religious experiences. Large numbers of converts to evangelism did remain socially conservative, seeing revivalism as the primary reform, salvation as the primary goal. But conversion to evangelism for some people crystallized already established reformist and humanitarian convictions.

For example, such different abolitionist leaders as William Lloyd Garrison, who interpreted the Constitution as a proslavery document and took an anti-political position; Theodore Dwight Weld, who would not fully align himself with the Garrisonians or the political abolitionists; and James G. Birney, a former slaveholder who was the abolitionist candidate for the presidency in 1840 and 1844, all shared important similarities that help to explain the ultimate appeal of immediatism for these men.

It had been impressed on Garrison and Weld by their strong, pious Christian mothers that to be good meant to do good. Birney was influenced in the same direction by his father and aunt. All the parents combined great affection for their children with intense concern for their children's salvation. And they provided appropriate models for future reformers through their pervasive concern with public service. Garrison's mother selflessly nursed the sick; Weld's father was a dedicated minister; and Birney's father was a state legislator who fought courageously for an end to slavery in his home state of Kentucky.

The power of evangelism to mold immediatist abolitionists seemed also to be limited to particular kinds of communities and certain social strata. While most abolitionist leaders were urban, the movement itself was most popular in moderately prosperous Yankee farming communities. Those portions of the country that retained genuine frontier conditions played little part in the movement, and the landed aristocracy of inherited wealth, Yankee or not, generally resisted immediate abolitionism (with Gerrit Smith a most notable exception). The converts to evangelism who were subsequently attracted to immediate abolitionism were most often secure and relatively substantial men and women who had previously displayed tendencies toward benevolent activity in their respective communities.

While the rise of immediatism was, at one level at least, a religious crusade, it was not a church movement. That most abolitionists were religious people did not mean that most religious people were abolitionists. In fact, the antislavery clergy, who were only a small proportion of the whole clergy, were generally unable to convert their churches to their views. Not until 1850 did the Northern New School Presbyterian Assembly, for example, adopt a resolution that slavery was "intrinsically an ... oppressive system opposed to the proscriptions of the law of God." The Congregational Church, under the influence of its leading clergyman, Horace Bushnell, who was explicitly anti-black, generally supported colonization.

No Methodist bishops took an aggressive stand against slavery. Moreover, in 1836, a General Conference of Methodist Churchmen adopted a resolution disapproving "in the most unqualified sense the conduct of two members [Orange Scott and La Roy Sunderland] who are reported to have lectured ... in favor of modern abolitionism." And a declaration in 1834 urging immediate emancipation received the signatures of only eleven Baptist ministers in all of New York and New England.

Abolitionism was rarely on the agenda at official Catholic or Episcopal gatherings; in fact, there was a total lack of abolitionist activity within Catholicism, possibly because of the minority status of Catholics and their fear of embarrassing the church, which supported what it saw as a benevolent slavery in Latin America. Most Lutheran ministers believed that reform was not a proper subject of discussion for an ecclesiastical body. These churches were dominated, not by proslavery elements, but by men who thought that anything but neutrality on "political" questions was improper for a religious group. Other churchmen attacked slavery but would not support the abolitionist movement.

The church establishment was generally interested in the preservation of the Union and of their national churches. The pressure to maintain denominational unity was strong. In an era when the issues of temperance, women's rights, and the nature of the Divinity were already burning the ties of many American denominations, most clergy did not want to add the fuel of the slavery question to the fire.

Thus abolitionists and the abolitionist clergy were often caught in the dilemma of belonging to churches that indirectly condoned slavery. Generally unable to convert their churches to abolitionism, the antislavery advocates, especially in the 1840's, often withdrew or, to use their own biblical expression, "came out." Some subsequently formed "abolitionist churches"—usually free, nonsectarian, Christian Union churches with a large degree of local autonomy. Others, especially the followers of William Lloyd Garrison, remained outside official church organization altogether.

Beyond evangelism, another important direct stimulus to immediatism in American abolitionism was the successful emancipation of 1 million slaves in the British West Indies. While the British emancipation plan adopted in 1831 provided for eight years of apprenticeship prior to complete freedom for the ex-slave and £20,000,000 in compensation to the slaveholders, the plan did end slavery. And it came only after the British abolitionists in 1831 officially adopted the posture and tactics of immediatism.

The example was not lost on American abolitionists. Lydia Maria Child, the editor of the New York weekly *National Anti-*

slavery Standard, insisted that the British West Indies experience proved the value of immediatism over halfway measures. And the Methodist minister La Roy Sunderland asked his colleagues in the abolitionist crusade why they were "so far behind our Brethren in England in relation to this thing."

British abolitionists could also now turn more of their attention to America to reinforce an immediatism that was already growing there. In Britain as in America, immediatism was the result, in part, of evangelism, demonstrating the powerful religious component in the trans-Atlantic abolitionist movement. The annual Conference of British Wesleyans in 1834 expressed chagrin that slavery and the "sinfully degrading caste of colour" were still maintained anywhere and asked that professedly Christian America follow the example of Great Britain in wiping out the "abominations." British Baptists and Methodists contributed to the antislavery stimulus by exerting direct pressure upon their American coreligionists. British Presbyterians toured the Northern United States in 1834 making "kind, brotherly exhortations to oppose slavery." And Britishers Joseph John Gurney and Joseph Sturge pleaded with American Quakers to revive the antislavery energies of their fathers. For while large numbers of individual Quakers participated in immediatism, as a group they shied away from it because of the "premeditated preaching of the abolitionists" and the fiery abolitionist agitation which Quakers viewed as covert violence.

George Thompson, perhaps England's most militant abolitionist, helped to organize several Methodist abolitionist societies in America. He converted Orange Scott, a prominent American Methodist minister, to immediate abolitionism. Scott subsequently led 6,000 Methodist abolitionists out of the Methodist Church and helped to create a new denomination, the antislavery Wesleyan Methodist Church.

Immediatism in America, then, was the result of the larger society's refusal to plan for gradual emancipation, the growth of black militancy, evangelical revivalism, the successful example of British emancipation, and, to some extent, encouragement by British abolitionists. Once immediatism had emerged, it was reinforced by the rhetoric of American democracy, which in the 1830's and 1840's was giving many Americans the inspiration and energy to strive for a better life. The committed abolitionist asked how such repressive institutions as American slavery and racial discrimination could be justified in a society whose ideological underpinnings were liberty, equality, and individual freedom and opportunity. Armed with their new commitment, immediatists attempted to convince Christians of their guilt and Americans in general of their hypocrisy. They hoped to create a new consciousness that would liberate the inner moral forces of human nature and bring on a new epoch of history.

4. Moral Suasion

The American Anti-Slavery Society was founded in Philadelphia in 1833 by a group of about fifty abolitionists from ten states. Their aim was to help abolitionists throughout the country carry out the unfinished work of the American Revolution—freeing the nation from slavery and racial discrimination. Abolitionists would proceed without violence, they said, using only "moral suasion" to effect their ends. Members of the American Anti-Slavery Society would work, according to their Declaration of Sentiments, for "the destruction of error by the potency of truth—the overthrow of prejudice by the power of love—and the abolition of slavery by the spirit of repentance."

Until about 1837, abolitionists agreed that moral suasion, not coercion, was indeed the best and most noble avenue to the destruction of slavery. Most abolitionists then believed that in order to achieve significant and enduring change, powerful appeals to conscience would have to be the central aspect of the abolitionist crusade and coercive tactics would have to be kept to a minimum. They recognized that legal changes alone were often ineffective. Nathaniel P. Rogers, a New Hampshire abolitionist, said that legal changes in the North had done no more than transform the slave there into a "free nigger." Where, Rogers asked, is the liberty of the black man who has been emancipated by the magic force of politics in the Northern states? New York, for example, "has abolished slavery by *law*; yet it [is] as much as a colored man's life is worth to live in her cities."

Abolitionists understood that man's social situation strongly influenced his values and his goals. They recognized that slavery had a powerful impact on the Southerner's view of the black as an inferior being and that many Southerners accommodated the "peculiar institution" in their midst by developing a view of themselves as a socially necessary master class. Abolitionists knew, therefore, that change might take more than moral suasion. Even the redoubtable moral suasionist Garrison wrote, in 1840,

> There is not an instance recorded, either in sacred or profane history, in which the oppressors and enslavers of mankind, except in individual cases, have been induced, by mere moral suasion, to surrender their despotic power, and let the oppressed go free.

But abolitionists rejected the idea that man is the simple creature of circumstance. They thought that this denied man's responsibility for his actions. By emphasizing individual responsibility, abolitionists hoped they could move men to transcend their social context by sheer will. They believed, perhaps naïvely, that men could break their own chains as well as those binding their slaves.

Prejudice and slavery were seen as twin products of an unregenerate soul. But slaveholders and racists were not merely sinners; they were men and as such, they were thought to be perfectible. The conversion of slaveholders, racists, and the indifferent through moral suasion would generate love of all men as brothers, or so the abolitionists hoped. This would create the will to abolish slavery and to make the black an equal in American society.

Moral suasion included all tactics short of overt coercion and violence, and aimed at developing in America a moral disposition to see slavery as evil. By 1840 the Garrisonians and the political abolitionists had developed significant tactical and ideological differences. But their respective means and ends were not mutually exclusive, and most abolitionists in both camps continued throughout the antebellum period to see moral suasion at least as a significant strategy.

For the Garrisonians, moral suasion was more than a strategy.

They understood that the cause of slavery was not the incidental, temporary seizure of blacks but the ancient and pervasive acceptance of the right of some men to coerce others. Thus many Garrisonians were nonresistants and strong supporters of women's rights as well as abolitionists. Nonresistance meant the renunciation of *all* coercive, authoritarian relationships among people. Most Garrisonians could not, then, coerce people to give up their slaves. Forced emancipation would not significantly alter human relationships. On the other hand, to convince people that coercion, whether physical, political, or social, was inhuman and ungodly would foster a generally revolutionary change in the way people lived as well as rid America of the specific evil of slavery.

The political abolitionists viewed much of their activity as educational rather than coercive. Therefore they did not perceive themselves as having abandoned moral suasion as a strategy. They seemed preoccupied, however, with specifically abolishing slavery and ending racial discrimination. Indeed, they thought it was essential for the American Anti-Slavery Society and its auxiliaries to be officially conservative on all subjects other than abolition. And in order to make abolitionism more respectable, several political abolitionists explicitly attempted to separate the movement from Garrison by splitting with him in 1840 and repudiating what were then called "ultraisms," such as nonresistance and women's rights. Although they sometimes pursued other reforms individually, the political abolitionists, including Lewis Tappan, James G. Birney, and Gerrit Smith, failed to see as clearly as the Garrisonians had that all the problems were intimately related and could not be divorced one from another.

The differences between the two groups were important, but they also had much in common. All the abolitionists were radical reformers. They all opted for an extreme course—the elimination of hundreds of thousands of dollars' worth of property and the transformation of that property into millions of new citizens. This goal could be attained only by overturning the power base of the Southern neo-aristocracy, and by shifting power drastically in the North. The political abolitionists were more willing to use the "system" than the Garrisonians were, but both groups rejected gradualism, which simply postponed serious thought about the question of slavery.

Most abolitionists in both groups recognized the brutalizing effect of slavery on the white master as well as on the black chattel. And the environmentalism inherent in this view represented a radical advance over the overt paternalism of the previous era. Both groups of abolitionists were concerned with the happiness and perfectibility of mankind. While neither group paid much attention to the implicit exploitative relationships within capitalism, they shared the radical aim of at least reducing the arbitrary power, authoritarianism, and coercion current in human existence.

Therefore, the activities and aims of the Garrisonians, who generally worked outside of institutions, often reinforced those of the non-Garrisonians, who generally worked through political parties or churches. Moreover, there were moral suasion actions even after 1840 in which Garrisonians and political abolitionists directly cooperated.

As historian Carleton Mabee (1970) has demonstrated, all groups of abolitionists right up to the eve of the Civil War tried a variety of nonpolitical, moral-suasion approaches to reform, including the direct action of sit-ins, ride-ins, and boycotts. Their general aims were to end racial discrimination in specific instances and to awaken consciences North and South on the slavery question. The two aims were intimately related. Political abolitionist William Goodell, editor of the New York paper *Friend of Man*, believed that as long as Northern laws, institutions, and customs rendered "the freedom of the colored people but an empty name—but the debasing mockery of true freedom," it would be difficult for abolitionists to condemn Southern practices. Massachusetts abolitionist Elizur Wright, Jr., exclaimed that if "every man take his stand, turn out this prejudice, live it down, talk it down, everywhere consider the colored man as a man, in the church, the stage, the steamboat, the public house, in all places, . . . the death blow to slavery will be struck."

Many abolitionists believed that by fighting for racial integration on moral grounds they could attack the conscience of a complacent white majority and move it in the direction of abolition. They also believed that even limited successes in desegregation would soon demonstrate black equality and help to destroy the myths supporting racial separation and slavery. When white consciousness about blacks was brought to a new sensitivity and awareness, slavery, it was believed, would collapse under the weight of moral criticism, and freedmen would in turn be inducted into full citizenship.

The abolitionists faced immense obstacles. Racism, as historian George Frederickson (1971) has persuasively suggested, was increasing in America as the nineteenth century advanced. Americans were not ethnically rooted in the land they inhabited, and their society was marked by flux and constant change. Apparently this unstable situation led whites to see blacks as a foil for their own elusive identity—as anti-Caucasians. If whites could not define who they were, the blacks at least defined who they were *not*. The mid-nineteenth century also saw the development of what Frederickson calls *Herrenvolk* egalitarianism, a perspective that regarded whites as equal to one another, at least in their common superiority to blacks. This concept was used by ultrademocrats as well as by elites in both sections of the country, who attempted to persuade deprived and frustrated whites that (despite much evidence to the contrary) they were as equal as anyone.

A more benign but no less reactionary form of race prejudice was also making itself felt at this time. This was a romantic racism, apparently a European import growing out of the emerging nationalisms there, which ascribed unique inherent qualities to various "national" groups.

Unfortunately, as recent historians have emphasized, white abolitionists themselves were not wholly free of the racial prejudice that permeated American society. They could paternalistically describe blacks as "genial . . . docile . . . in whom the affections rule . . . and who overflow with the exuberance of childhood." Yet a great many white abolitionists fully believed in the inherent equality of the races, and the vast majority, whatever their racial beliefs, supported economic and political equality for blacks. And even though some abolitionists thought social relations with blacks "unwise," others did pursue them.

Unlike the mass black demonstrations of the 1940's and 1950's and the collective student sit-ins of the 1960's, the nineteenth-century battle against prejudice most often consisted of individual acts by black and white abolitionists. The black abolitionist minister Charles B. Ray and fugitive slaves William Wells Brown and Frederick Douglass all bravely faced threats of violence and arrest in order to ride under equal conditions with whites on steamboats. Frederick Douglass, the self-educated fugitive slave and future Minister to Haiti, was undoubtedly the most important black abolitionist. His reform career spanned more than five decades, and he was a man of enormous courage and intellect. An important part of Douglass' strategy was to act as though prejudice did not exist and to associate with his "fellow creatures irrespective of all complexional differences. We have marked out this path for ourselves," he wrote, "and we mean to pursue it at all hazards."

Occasionally, whole groups acted against discrimination. At Alliance, Ohio, in 1852, Douglass, on his way to the National Convention of the Free Soil party, was refused service in the dining room of a hotel. The abolitionist delegates to the convention stopped at Alliance on their way home and pointedly boycotted the hotel dining room, which had prepared several hundred meals in anticipation of the stopover.

William Lloyd Garrison and a party of abolitionists, including the black Robert Purvis, boycotted segregated public transportation in their trips between Philadelphia and New York. They believed, Garrison wrote in *The Liberator*, that if their action was "extensively imitated by antislavery men . . . every barrier of caste [would] soon be overthrown."

In 1840 the American Anti-Slavery Society arranged for delegates, black and white, to dine together during its annual meeting in New York. Although a mob made some trouble over this integrated meal, by the end of the decade the American and Foreign Anti-Slavery Society (organized by the Tappans after splitting with Garrison in 1840) held interracial breakfasts in New York without disturbance.

The actions against racial discrimination, however, were most often spontaneous, individual, and short-lived. For example, white abolitionists sometimes boarded with black families. Augustus Wattles chose to do so in Cincinnati, while teaching black children there; and Theodore Weld lived at editor Samuel Cornish's home in New York when he was working at the American Anti-Slavery Society office on the grand project of collecting a host of agents to abolitionize the country. And when white abolitionists traveled, they sometimes stayed with black families during their stopovers. Garrison often stopped at Charles Remond's house in Salem, Massachusetts; the young Unitarian minister Samuel J. May was put up at the Fortens' in Philadelphia. Traveling blacks dined or stayed overnight with Garrison in Boston, or with Gerrit Smith in Peterboro.

In 1841, some abolitionists attempted to organize direct action, hoping to involve large numbers of people more deeply. At a meeting of the Massachusetts Anti-Slavery Society, abolitionists discussed what they should do about segregated railroads. Stephen S. Foster, a former Congregational minister, proposed the following resolution:

> We recommend to [white] abolitionists as the most consistent and effectual method of abolishing the 'Negro-pew,' to take their seats in it, wherever it may be found, whether in a . . . [church], a railroad car, a steamboat, or a stagecoach.

The Massachusetts Society did not approve Foster's resolution or organize any collective action, but they did require that members protest against segregation and work "in some way" to abolish it. Some individuals chose the "ride-in" method in their attempt to desegregate public transportation. Massachusetts was a good target. In this state, unlike most Northern states, blacks served on juries, voted, and attended public schools with whites. Most seating in public transportation here was already desegregated. Abolitionists hoped to extend desegregation to the railroads. Ultimately fifty adults took part in the railroad "ride-ins," including Wendell Phillips and Quaker James N. Buffum. Most of the time white abolitionists attempted to sit in black sections of trains. They were generally beaten up or at least pushed around by railroad employees. Sometimes black abolitionists tried to ride in white sections of railroad cars and trains. Mrs. Mary Green, Secretary of the Lynn Female Anti-Slavery Society, sat in the white area of the Eastern Railroad. The conductor dragged her out, and although she was holding an infant, she was struck and thrown to the ground. When her husband attempted to aid her, several employees of the railroad beat him severely. Abolitionists, irrespective of color, learned to expect rough treatment when they rode-in.

Their suffering helped to convince some of the public of their sincerity and won abolitionists a hearing. In this way, Buffum believed, ride-ins were not only helping to end segregation but were stimulating the abolitionist movement generally. "In Lynn, it has been the means of bringing new converts to the cause . . . people are roused into active discussion."

The Massachusetts abolitionists, including some Garrisonians, escalated their challenges with a boycott of segregated railroads and an appeal to the state legislature to require equal rights for blacks in all conveyances chartered by Massachusetts. Pain of conscience, nuisance, loss of business, and threat of legislation made a powerful combination, and by 1843 the railroads "voluntarily" desegregated.

Churches were a primary target for all abolitionists. The Garrisonians were as convinced as the political abolitionists "that there is no power out of the Church that could maintain Slavery, if the Church attacked it in earnest." Both abolitionist groups probably attached more importance to the reformation of churches than to any other aspect of the cause.

The first step in the reformation was the attempt to break up the traditional seating pattern. Frederick Douglass urged blacks to attend white churches in massive pray-ins and to refuse to sit in "Negro-pews" in racially mixed churches. While a substantial number of individual blacks followed Douglass' advice, no collective, sustained pray-in by the black community developed. And those blacks who did "pray-in" generally met with frustration.

A black Massachusetts family purchased a pew in a Baptist church with an otherwise all-white congregation. One Sunday, they found the pew had been removed. The family sat bravely on the floor. The next Sunday, they found the flooring removed. The family stood through the service. Similar frustration faced two black brothers who stopped attending Friends meetings because, as one said, "I do not like to sit on a back bench and be treated with contempt."

White abolitionists, including Samuel J. May, also made efforts in the direction of abolishing the "Negro-pew." May was a pastor with little interest in expounding systematic theology; his ambition was to convert men to the life of personal righteousness. Therefore, May was very active in the movement for universal peace and women's rights in addition to black liberation. May once invited Angelina Grimké, a former slaveholder, to occupy his pulpit and address his congregation on abolitionism; and he invited blacks to sit without restriction in his church in Connecticut. But during a time when May was off lecturing on abolitionism, the congregation arranged to move the blacks to the gallery. This was a skirmish in a long battle over abolitionism between the pastor and his church, which finally led May to resign.

After Angelina and her sister Sarah Grimké, the only Southern white women in the abolitionist movement, became Friends, they insisted on sitting with the black women in a Philadelphia meeting house. When scolded by whites for this, they replied, "While you put this badge of degradation on our sisters, we feel it is our duty to share it with them."

Because of white intransigence, there was much more support among blacks for withdrawal from churches with segregated seating than for invasion or disruption of those institutions. Yet there was some progress in reducing segregation. By the end of the 1840's, hundreds of churches had abolished the Negro-pew system, although most churches in the North still had segregated seating by the time of the Civil War. As in the second half of the 1960's, blacks who were frustrated by the ineffectiveness of integration as a liberating force sought control of their own institutions. The all-black church grew, becoming one of the strongest institutions of black society.

Education was another important target for abolitionists as well as for others who recognized the inhumanity of purposely keeping blacks ignorant. In the South, by 1830, black education was generally limited by custom and law to oral religious instruction. In the border state of Kentucky, a grand jury moved to break up a school for slaves, fearing that it would enlighten "the minds of those whose happiness obviously depends on their ignorance."

Angelina Grimké, in an "Appeal to the Christian Women of the South," called on her sisters to free their slaves, or pay them wages and educate them, even if the law forbade it—"such wicked laws ought to be no barrier in the way of your duty."

Mrs. Margaret Douglass, a white seamstress in Norfolk, Virginia, took Angelina seriously and ran a school for black children during the 1830's. When asked to leave town, Mrs. Douglass refused, saying she was willing to face punishment; she thought the law prohibiting black education was unjust and wanted a chance to say so openly. At her trial she denied being an abolitionist but charged that the law she had broken was one of the "most inhuman . . . laws that ever disgraced the statute books of a civilized community." She was jailed for one month. Upon her release Mrs. Douglass, fully aware of white hostility, moved North.

Education for blacks in the North, where it existed, was better than in the South, but it was grossly inferior to educational facilities for whites, and in most instances was segregated. In New England, the pattern varied from general acceptance of blacks in the school system of Maine to their general exclusion in Connecticut. Areas of New York State that had relatively heavy black populations set up separate public schools for blacks. And in the Western states, discrimination and segregation were generally quite severe.

Where Northern city systems accepted blacks, they invariably put them into inferior separate schools. This was true in the 1830's and 1840's in Boston, Providence, New York, Rochester, Buffalo, Philadelphia, and Pittsburgh. Even where blacks were in the same schools or classes with whites, black children faced discrimination and discouragement.

Abolitionists believed that "the education of the people of color . . . [was] a most important means of bringing about the abolition of slavery and the removal of . . . prejudice." Where they could, abolitionists invited blacks into white schools, or used petitions, court suits, and boycotts to end segregation, or created new schools that would accept blacks.

In Canterbury, Connecticut, in 1833, Prudence Crandall admitted a black child to her private girls' school. The white students did not object, but their irate parents withdrew their children. With the encouragement of William Lloyd Garrison, Miss Crandall thereupon turned her school into a learning institution for black girls, including out-of-state children.

The townspeople were intent on driving Miss Crandall and her school out. The Canterbury merchants refused to sell the school supplies; the town doctor refused to treat its pupils; and the church refused to admit them. Furthermore, townspeople persuaded the state legislature to pass a law requiring that schools teaching out-of-state pupils have town approval. Prudence Crandall defied the law and was arrested. Samuel J. May advised her to refuse bail money from friends so that she would be jailed. He explained to the sheriff: "The people generally will not so soon recognize how bad, how unkind, how cruel a law it is, unless we suffer her [Miss Crandall's] persecutors to inflict upon her all the penalties it prescribed. She is willing to bear them for the sake of the cause she has so nobly espoused." Miss Crandall continued, in defiance of the law, to operate the school after her release, until, in the summer of 1834, townspeople wielding iron bars attacked the building and attempted to burn it down. Apparently this action triggered a sympathetic response to Prudence Crandall's obvious sincerity. For in 1838, the Connecticut state legislature, influenced by some of the men who had originally persecuted her, repealed the law that had been passed to enable Canterbury whites to close Prudence Crandall's school.

In Canaan, New Hampshire, some Garrisonian abolitionists attempted to establish an interracial school. Townspeople there looked to no state legislature for help. They tore the school building from its foundations and dragged it into a swamp. The school was never reopened.

William C. Nell, a black Garrisonian abolitionist, believed that the violence against black and interracial schools had called attention to the barbaric exclusion of blacks from the American educational system. And, perhaps because of the reaction to violence here, New England schools and colleges in the late 1830's and 1840's opened their doors to blacks faster than in any other part of the country. By 1845, fourteen of the academies, colleges, and theological seminaries in New England—more than half the total—were known to be open to students of every complexion on the same terms.

Lewis Tappan and his abolitionist associates ran a highly successful interracial school, Oneida Institute in central New York. Tappan sent his own sons here; Theodore Dwight Weld, who wrote *Slavery as It Is*, the handbook of the abolitionist movement for more than a decade, studied here; and it was here that black abolitionists Henry Highland Garnet and Amos Beman were educated. Under the presidency of minister Beriah Green (1833–44), who was converted to abolitionism by Weld, Oneida Institute became the center for interracial education, abolitionism, and peace principles.

The Tappans also supported the interracial Lane Theological Seminary in Ohio. Lyman Beecher, who had been Garrison's pulpit idol in Boston, and who was passively antislavery, was persuaded to accept the presidency. Lane students, strongly influenced by Theodore Dwight Weld, eagerly espoused abolitionist convictions. When they implemented their convictions by working to educate blacks in Cincinnati, the trustees of the Seminary, in a classic instance of administrative overreaction, forbade them to continue this work or even to discuss slavery at the school. Fifty students, among them the future political abolitionist Henry B. Stanton, withdrew from the school and moved to Oberlin, a small, financially weak, manual-labor college. The Tappans and the students refounded Oberlin College on the principles of free discussion of controversial reforms and acceptance of blacks as students. Oberlin ultimately contributed more than any other college to the antebellum education of blacks.

Heartening as all this was, public schools for blacks were still, in the 1840's and 1850's, of very low quality. Despite abolitionist successes in integrating higher education, the great masses of blacks were unaffected. Only one major city in the nation—Boston—desegregated its public schools prior to the Civil War. This came after a comprehensive campaign by abolitionists, led by black Garrisonians.

Between 1844 and 1855, many blacks participated in a boycott of Boston's only black public school. Some black parents withdrew their children; others chose to change their residence. Many blacks without school-age children moved out of Boston in order to avoid paying taxes to support a segregated system.

Several blacks who did not share Garrison's scruples about the coercion of law also tried to get satisfaction through a judicial decision. They engaged the black lawyer Robert Morris and Massachusetts Senator Charles Sumner. Sumner argued before the court that segregated schools were unconstitutional under the equal-protection guarantees of the Massachusetts Constitution. In 1850, the state Supreme Court ruled that each local school system could decide for itself on the issue of segregation.

In 1851 and again in 1854, undeterred protesters turned to the state legislature with a series of petitions to make segregated schools illegal. Finally, in 1855, the legislature passed a law desegregating Boston city schools.

The desegregation law was the crowning achievement of the abolitionist crusade for interracial education. Moral suasion had been central. The boycotts had required personal sacrifices over long periods of time and had helped make clear to concerned observers the depth of feeling over the issue in the black community. But, as we have seen, it was also necessary to use the legislature.

Abolitionists acted not only to end discrimination in specific instances; they also acted directly to awaken consciences, North and South, on the slavery question. To this end, a boycott of slave produce was endorsed by nearly all abolitionists. The Quakers led in this movement, and for a time Quaker Benjamin Lundy dared to keep a free-produce store in slave-owning Baltimore. The American Anti-Slavery Society endorsed the boycott, and the liberal Quaker Lucretia Mott worked indefatigably to increase support.

Abolitionists believed that an extensive boycott of slave produce would accomplish three things: The individual crusader
would achieve self-purification through non-cooperation with
the system; the slaveholder's conscience would be affected; and
economic coercion might achieve the manumission of slaves.
While moral suasionists chose to disavow the inherent coercion
of a boycott, they at least recognized the potential effectiveness
of this element of the technique. (Many abolitionists knew that
after 800,000 Englishwomen had signed a pledge not to use
slave-grown sugar, there was a penny-per-pound drop in price,
which alarmed West Indian slaveowners.) And Benjamin Lundy
explicitly argued that no reform had ever been accomplished
merely by appeals to conscience.

But Elizur Wright, Jr., insisted that if the South were compelled to abolish slavery solely by consideration of interest,
reformation would be only minimal. And, indeed, most abolitionists avoided using the boycott for economic coercion. Instead,
they hoped, like Gerrit Smith, that an extensive "testimony of . . .
self-denial would carry more conviction to the minds of slaveholders of the truth and power of antislavery doctrines and of
the sincerity with which they are held." The boycott was ineffective. Many abolitionists did not participate in it, and those who
did often found it difficult to be consistent. Everywhere they
turned, some product somewhere along the line had been touched
by the slave system. Still, some abolitionists continued to argue
that a boycott would reach the Southern conscience.

Influential Southerners like Duff Green, editor of the authorita-
tive *United States Telegraph*, recognized and feared what these
abolitionists were trying to do to Southerners. Green wrote in
1836:

We believe that we have most to fear from the organized action
upon the CONSCIENCES and fears of the slaveholders themselves. . . .
It is only by alarming the *consciences* of the weak and feeble, and
diffusing among our own people a morbid sensibility on the question of slavery, that the abolitionists can accomplish their object.

Abolitionists, although often discouraged, never completely

gave up on the idea that moral suasion could work in the South. James G. Birney, the Grimké sisters, several of the Lane rebels, and other abolitionists were reformed slaveholders, and believed that many more could be induced to follow their path.

It was just as necessary to make whites in the North feel the reality of slavery and imagine themselves in the place of slaves. Beriah Green advised Northern men, including those abolitionists who reflected their society's prejudices, to

> ... act as if you felt that you were bound with those who are in bonds; as if their cause was all your own; as if every blow that cuts their flesh, lacerated yours. You can plead their cause with the earnestness, and zeal, and decision, which self-defense demands.

Angelina Grimké understood that "Northern prejudice . . . is grinding the colored man to the dust in our free states, and this is strengthening the hands of the oppressor continually." Northern whites, including abolitionists, would need to develop empathy to overcome this. Treat blacks as equals, Angelina advised. "Multitudes of instances will continually occur in which you will have the opportunity of *identifying yourself with this injured class* of our fellow beings; embrace these opportunities at all times and in all places."

Most abolitionists revealed awareness of the implications of prejudice. Their meetings were integrated, and they gave black members a chance to take leadership positions. Yet these actions were often the subject of intense debate during the 1830's, indicating that prejudice among abolitionists had not been completely destroyed.

Angelina Grimké, speaking for the female abolitionists, appealed to her "colored sisters":

> We are aware of the prejudice you suffer daily, but entreat you to bear with us in our folly. You must be willing to mingle with us whilst we have the prejudice, because it is only by associating with you that we shall be able to overcome it.

In their portrayal of slavery, abolitionists admitted that some slaveholders were motivated by humanitarian impulses, that in some cases masters treated slaves well and preached the Gospel to them; but in all cases the blacks were still slaves, and this fact alone, the abolitionists said, ran against the grain of freedom, human dignity, and Christian love. While abolitionists used exaggerated rhetoric—calling slavery a "legalized system of licentiousness," and broadcasting innumerable atrocity stories— they were quite correct in pointing out that all slaves were potentially helpless victims of the grossest exploitation.

In their attempt to eliminate racial discrimination, abolitionists had attacked the church for its segregation. In their attempt to awaken consciences, abolitionists attacked the church for its silence on slavery. In James G. Birney's words, the church was "the bulwark of slavery." Like the more modern black militant Eldridge Cleaver, many abolitionists believed that a person or institution that was not part of the solution was part of the problem.

One Sunday morning in 1841, during a pause in the service at the Congregational Church in Concord, New Hampshire, Stephen Foster denounced that church for upholding slavery. Foster refused to stop speaking and was taken by the arms and led out. Undaunted, the fiery New Hampshire abolitionist returned to the afternoon service for a repeat performance. This time he was thrown down the stairs and arrested for disturbing the peace. Foster was to be arrested some dozen times more in his career, as well as thrown out of many windows and dragged out of innumerable churches.

Stephen Foster's actions were seen by many abolitionists, including Garrison, as too coercive and needlessly offensive. However, apparently Foster never interrupted a service unless he had first tried and failed to win a hearing. And he did gain a following, though small, among abolitionists.

Thomas P. Beach, a Congregational minister, joined Foster in the work of speak-ins. Others simply followed his example. Maria French of Salem, Massachusetts, spoke-in and then withdrew from membership in the local Congregational Church. In Georgetown, Massachusetts, Mrs. Elmira Sweet was arrested for a Foster-style disruption. The Georgetown jailer was apparently affected by the moral power of Mrs. Sweet's action, because he refused to receive her, declaring that those who sent her were more deserving of arrest. Abby Kelly, a Quaker-reared school-teacher who later married Stephen Foster, was another who became actively involved in speak-ins, in which she demonstrated remarkable articulateness.

More popular than speaking-in was the call that all churches exclude slaveholders from communion. In 1834 the American Anti-Slavery Society officially endorsed this policy. And, according to Frederick Douglass, the idea had "become very prevalent in the free states." Some congregations refused to accept slaveholders as ministers. And men sometimes turned down pastorates because the congregation included slaveholders. John G. Fee, abolitionist Presbyterian pastor, did this in Kentucky, where he subsequently established a number of antislavery churches.

Many abolitionists, Garrisonian or not, supported withdrawal from proslavery churches. The political-abolitionist leader, William Goodell, for example, asked whether the abolitionists who stayed in a proslavery church were influencing the church's position or being influenced by it.

A number of Methodist ministers asked themselves the same question and answered it by withdrawing from their churches. After abolitionists had been persecuted by American citizens, North and South, between 1837 and 1843, thousands of Methodist congregants withdrew to form the Wesleyan Methodist Church. These "come-outer" Methodists, with financial help from Lewis Tappan, were able to spread as far as the middle South, securing a precarious foothold even in places like North Carolina. Despite, or perhaps because of, the fact that they were harassed, imprisoned, and in some cases murdered in North Carolina, their numbers increased from forty in 1846 to five hundred in 1851.

Followers of Lewis Tappan also tried to abolitionize church-related organizations, such as the American Bible Society and the American Home Missionary Society. But in 1846, after a series of setbacks, Tappan and others took the lead in creating a new, distinctly antislavery missionary society—the American Missionary Association. The Association's aim was to convert the South. It insisted that churches must be open to blacks and whites equally and must not permit slaveholders to be members.

In Kentucky, John G. Fee, a leader in the Association's missionary effort, created several interracial grade schools as well as Berea College (1855), dedicated to racial justice. By mid-1859, the Association was working in the slaveholding areas of Kentucky, Missouri, North Carolina, and the District of Columbia.

The effect of this direct action on Southern consciences was mixed. Abolitionists were mobbed, poisoned, and hanged in the South. Fee, despite his gentle appeals and Kentucky birth, was beaten up twenty-two times. But in some instances, persecution strengthened the cause. By the eve of the Civil War, there were several outposts of abolitionism in the Upper South slave states, including five antislavery schools and twenty-one antislavery churches. Over all, however, Southern churchmen grew more defensive about their peculiar institution and developed more elaborate proslavery arguments as time went on.

In the North, the attack on the church led to large numbers of withdrawals, but no major denominations were transformed into abolitionist agencies. As late as 1853, abolitionist pastor Theodore Parker wrote to his Unitarian colleague Samuel J. May:

> The American pulpit is the sworn ally of slavery. . . . I know there are exceptional pulpits . . . but how few they are!—little lamps hung out from windows, here and there on a country road at night, they only show how deep the darkness is.

Another kind of moral suasion used in an attempt to awaken consciences was the call for voluntary dissolution of the Union. Wendell Phillips, for example, said:

> To propose a dissolution of the Union is the best way of holding up such a mirror to the national mind, as makes it to see its own deformity. . . . Disunion startles a man to thought. It takes a lazy abolitionist by the throat, and thunders in his ear, *"Thou* art the slaveholder."

Abolitionists called for disunion as they had called for immediate emancipation. It was a call for psychological and social, more than political, separation, a call that they knew could not be immediately translated into practice. It was the statement of a moral imperative, a call to conscience.

Garrison, for example, attempted to explain that it was not primarily a demand for a physical or political separation of the free from the slave states. "The appeal," he wrote,

> was not a geographical one, but is addressed to every individual who professes to abhor slavery, wherever he resides on American soil. . . . It has nothing sectional in its spirit or design, any further than one portion of the country may be more disposed to give heed to it than another, owing to a difference in the moral and intellectual condition of the inhabitants.

Disunion was based on the idea that the U. S. Constitution was a proslavery document. The Constitution allowed slavery in the states; it also contained a fugitive-slave clause and a three-fifths clause, indirectly recognizing the right to hold slaves. Several American leaders, including John Quincy Adams, had maintained as early as 1820 that the Constitution was proslavery, and the followers of John C. Calhoun had for a long time articulated this interpretation. Garrisonians came to their proslavery interpretation only in the 1840's, after they realized that the slave interests had no intention of allowing constitutional guarantees of liberty to be enforced—for slaves, for free blacks, or for abolitionists. As Univeralist clergyman Adin Ballou said, it was not until abolitionists "themselves were outlawed, mobbed and murdered, in shameless violation of every guarantee to liberty contained in the federal and state constitutions, that they were gradually driven to denounce the Constitution and Union as hopelessly sold to proslavery."

In 1845 William Jay called for disunion over the annexation of Texas, which he believed demonstrated the slave power's control over the federal government. He appealed to the North to protect its interests by seceding from the South. But Garrison's call was more an agitational weapon. In fact, disunionist agitation was justified by Garrisonians as the only way to save the Union. Abolition of slavery, they believed, was the only way to prevent the Union's dissolution, and disunionist agitation was the most effective way of working for abolition.

Disunionism was the most extreme part of a broader moral-suasion crusade—that of non-cooperation with government. Non-cooperation included the refusal to vote, hold office, participate in political parties, or hunt fugitive slaves. When it appeared that there would be war with Mexico, the Garrisonian Massachusetts Anti-Slavery Society called for citizens to sign a pledge that they would not "countenance or aid the United States government in any war . . . designed to strengthen or perpetuate slavery."

While the political abolitionists sometimes denounced the Garrisonian policy of non-cooperation with government as threatening to the social order, they joined the Garrisonians in denouncing the Mexican War. The newspapers of the political abolitionists overwhelmingly opposed the war. Lewis Tappan and Gerrit Smith called the war "folly and wickedness." And many political abolitionists joined the Garrisonians in asking Congress not to vote for war supplies.

Some abolitionists extended their non-cooperation with government to include non-payment of taxes. Henry David Thoreau, in the most celebrated case, refused, beginning in 1837, to pay taxes to a proslavery government. But Garrison, for one, advised paying taxes, and generally abolitionists paid them.

For some abolitionists, non-cooperation with government, including non-voting and disunion, was part of their philosophy of nonresistance, which saw all government as coercive and hence immoral. For others, non-cooperation was an attempt to free themselves of the contamination of a government which they believed was hopelessly under the control of the slave interests. But most abolitionists adopted non-cooperation as an agitational device. Garrison advised non-cooperation as a temporary antislavery tactic although he himself believed that the Union was inherently coercive, with or without slavery.

Moral suasion, as we have seen, was not a collection of naïve sermons on brotherhood. The abolitionists were tough. They ran an unremitting propaganda offensive against white consciences; they sat-in, prayed-in, and spoke-in to break the barriers of caste;

they sought to persuade the slaveholders and their Northern allies of the abolitionists' sincerity by disrupting economic, social, and religious relationships, and by risking, and facing, legal punishment as well as mob "reprisal."

But, as we have also seen, the direct actions of the moral-suasion approach were usually unorganized and fitful, aimed mostly at peripheral targets, such as segregated transportation, instead of more vital areas, such as discrimination in employment. Thus, while the moral suasionists had some effect in awakening Northerners to the injustice of slavery and bringing about minor improvements in the plight of Northern blacks— e.g., integrated transportation, higher education, and public schools—they did not reach the slaveholders, nor did they significantly alleviate the severity of racial discrimination.

By 1840, most abolitionists had already come to believe that moral suasion alone was ineffective. They turned, some optimistically, most reluctantly, to politics.

5. Escalating the Campaign:
Politics and Violence

We appealed to Congress and she threw us back our petitions, mixed with broken fragments of the Constitution. We have appealed to the slaveholder! He points to the . . . [whip]. We have tried the . . . system of questioning the political candidates in this land, hoping by that lever to pry open the prison doors,—We never, by this course, gained truth an advocate, or humanity a friend.—ALVAN STEWART, 1839

Rather than see men wearing their chains in a cowardly and servile spirit, I would, as an advocate of peace, much rather see them breaking the head of the tyrant with their chains.—WILLIAM LLOYD GARRISON, 1859

In the early years of their movement, abolitionists gave little thought to its political implications. Members of the American Anti-Slavery Society were pledged "to endeavor, in a constitutional way," to influence Congress both to abolish the interstate slave trade and to end slavery in the District of Columbia and the territories. Between 1833 and 1839 most abolitionists fulfilled this pledge by petitioning, interrogating candidates, and voting. Even the non-voting Garrisonians participated in petition campaigns to end slavery in U. S. territories and encouraged abolitionists who would vote to try to achieve a political balance of power through write-in campaigns.

There was also in the early years a revulsion against highly organized political action. This was part of the general preference for moral suasion. It also reflected a wish to avoid the appearance that the abolitionists were seeking their own selfish ends—e.g., the emoluments of office—in their adherence to the movement.

But when in the late 1830's moral suasion increasingly appeared to be ineffective, some abolitionists believed it necessary to move the slavery question into the political arena in an organized way. Many abolitionists who later led in political action were initially reluctant. For example, Gerrit Smith, future gubernatorial and presidential candidate of the abolitionist Liberty party, said in 1838 that the sole job of the abolitionists was to "publish the truth about slavery." Later that year, however, Smith associated himself with Myron Holley, who had already had a long career in public affairs, and Alvan Stewart, a leading New York lawyer, in initiating what they saw as a strategy to achieve political balance of power.

Smith agreed to ask a series of questions of New York political leaders in order to determine which candidates abolitionists should support at the polls. The questions appeared in the abolitionist newspaper *Emancipator* (Oct. 30, 1838) as follows:

Are you in favor of granting trial by jury to persons in New York claimed as fugitive slaves?

Do you favor the removal of all distinctions which are "founded solely on complexion" in the constitutional rights of citizens of New York?

Do you favor repeal of the law which now makes it possible for persons to bring slaves into New York and hold them there for not more than nine months?

Outside of New York, abolitionists asked similar questions emphasizing the dilemma of the free black. For example, Dr. Arthur Livermore Porter, a leading Michigan abolitionist, was delegated in 1839 to ask the following questions of office-seekers in his state:

> Are you in favor of removing from our State Constitution the article which makes color a condition of the right of the suffrage . . .?
>
> [And are you in favor of securing] to *all* persons, irrespective of color, the right of trial by jury in all questions?

Not surprisingly, abolitionists usually received evasive and unsatisfactory answers from politicians. No major party candidate wished to identify himself openly with an abolitionist, pro-black position when relatively few voters cared positively and intensely about this issue. Any gains the office-seeker might acquire by satisfying abolitionists would be offset by his losses from antagonizing anti-abolitionists.

By late 1839 some abolitionists admitted that the questioning technique was a failure and called for the nomination of abolitionist candidates independent of the major parties. Alvan Stewart contended, "If we ever strike a political blow for the slave we must go deep." And in October, 1839, Holley introduced a resolution that was passed at the Monroe County (New York) Anti-Slavery Convention calling for the creation of an abolitionist party. He continued to labor in behalf of that goal and was soon joined by such notable abolitionists as Henry B. Stanton, Alvan Stewart, and Joshua Leavitt, a Yale graduate and a lawyer who took up the editorship of *The Emancipator* (New York and Boston), a paper he personally turned into the leading organ for the expression of political abolitionism. (It is interesting to note that Leavitt, an ordained minister, was previously the editor of *The Evangelist,* which fostered religious revivalism and abolitionism.)

As the movement for political action gained force, Lewis Tappan, who was later to join and lead the political abolitionists, was uncompromising in his support of the old policy of questionnaires and petitions. He insisted that politics corrupted even the most sincere reformers and that a third party would alienate abolitionists who were apolitical. In fact, he observed, the abolitionists "are disunited already. There will probably be an abolition political party—a religious association—a Garrison party, &c. &c." He wrote to one of his brothers, Congressman Benjamin Tappan, "I have little confidence in the abiding and true-hearted abolitionism of any devotee to politics. Party, party, party! is the watchword, and moral questions are lost sight of too frequently."

In 1840 William Jay declined the New York gubernatorial nomination of the nascent Liberty party because he disapproved of "any further organized interference by abolitionists with elections than the official questioning of candidates." He thought that voting for third-party candidates would deprive major parties "of the little salt that keeps them from utter putrefaction."

Many other abolitionists resisted the third-party idea because the new party would take an explicit position on only one question—slavery. These men were not ready to abandon their concern for tariffs, internal improvements, and other issues of the day on which the major parties took strong positions.

But as the major parties continued to ignore the abolitionists, the reformers increasingly felt disfranchised, and by late 1840 the Liberty party was formed. What choice was there for them, after all, between the Democrat Martin Van Buren, who was publicly pledged to veto any bill to abolish slavery in the District of Columbia, and the Whig William Henry Harrison, who met contemporary issues by bragging about his record in the War of 1812? More and more abolitionists became frustrated by the intransigence of the major parties on the slavery question. Liberty party voters increased from about 7,000 in 1840 to about 62,000 in 1844.

The Liberty party's central mission was to make slavery the overriding issue of American politics. The hope was that the party could gain adherents without losing moral purpose. The abolitionists did not expect to do this by winning office but through a balance-of-power strategy that would force at least one of the major parties to take account of abolitionist sentiment. New York lawyer E. W. Clarke wrote to Alvan Stewart, "If you should get but one hundred votes for your ticket, that small number would probably turn the question and satisfy one of the parties that you had beaten it; even without victory, you will have success." And Henry B. Stanton attributed local New York Democratic victories to abolitionist defections from the Whigs to the Liberty party. He wrote to Gerrit Smith in 1840, "We have had a triumph. The Whig . . . candidates . . . spent weeks and hundreds to carry their point. . . . Their whole ticket is defeated."

In important respects the methods and goals of organized political action were similar to those of moral suasion. Denying the Whigs and Democrats votes by obtaining votes for a third party was no more coercive than the write-in device used by voting Garrisonians, who regarded themselves as moral-suasion men. And, like the Garrisonians, Liberty party men agreed that the two major parties were corrupt and servants of the slave power. Working and voting for the Liberty party was therefore seen as a way of working against the sinful parties rather than for coercive legislation.

Founders of the Liberty party saw it as a temporary vehicle of conversion. It would not only force the major parties to make antislavery concessions in an attempt to attract abolitionists back to the fold; it would demonstrate that significant numbers of men felt strongly enough about slavery to desert their parties, in an era of phenomenal party loyalty, in the hope that this would awaken consciences. Moral-suasion abolitionists used the same rationale in their withdrawal from churches, their refusal to give Christian fellowship to slaveholders, and their boycotts of slave produce.

Men who moved abolitionism into politics in the 1840's were initially motivated not so much by the possibility of electing antislavery candidates as by the fear that revivalism and its concomitant concern for social justice had reached a plateau and were in danger of diminishing. Abolitionism had to be kept in the forefront of American consciousness. And since politics was a passionate national pastime in mid-nineteenth-century America, abolitionists entered the political arena.

Yet even here the abolitionists emphasized suasion rather than coercion. The Liberty party carried on a propaganda offensive to convince Southern state legislatures to abolish slavery. But the party program did not call for Congress to abolish slavery in the states, and it did not push enthusiastically for an end to the interstate slave trade. It asked Congress to end slavery only at its periphery—in the territories.

The party, in an attempt to increase its audience, did try to educate Northerners to believe in the aggressions of a "slave power" which controlled the national government to the interest of the South and misfortune of the North. It may therefore have inadvertently helped to develop an antislavery constituency— i.e., voters who were centrally concerned with slavery's negative effect on white America's economic and political life rather than with slavery's effect on the blacks victimized by the institution and on the whites who administered it. But the party program in the 1840's demanded equal rights for blacks as intensely as it attempted to demonstrate the existence of a slavocracy detrimental to American institutions. And the party literature constantly and centrally attacked slavery as morally wrong. Thus, in many ways, the political abolitionists were carrying on the work of moral suasion in a more visible context.

The early political abolitionists, like other moral suasionists, recognized their classic role as agitators. For a long time, they were only incidentally concerned with the art of the possible; their focus was on raising the consciousness of large numbers of people in order to facilitate significant social transformation.

Moreover, Garrison himself recognized that abolition would ultimately come at the ballot box, "renovating the political action of the country . . . stirring up the torpid consciences of voters . . . modifying and rescinding all laws which sanction slavery." And he never opposed the Liberty party as wrong in principle. Garrison wrote in *The Liberator*:

> We have never opposed the formation of a third party as a measure inherently wrong, . . . abolitionists have as clear and indisputable [a] right to band themselves together politically . . . as . . . their fellow-citizens who call themselves whigs or democrats.

Garrison did object to the Liberty party, however, because he felt that it was "not the best mode to advance the antislavery cause." He believed that voting abolitionists should work through (though not for) both parties in order to abolitionize them and thought that withdrawal into a third party, which both major parties could ignore, would be ineffective. Just as important, Garrison and Lewis Tappan, even after Tappan had joined the political abolitionists, doubted that Liberty men would remain "true to their principles." The dynamic of direct political participation would prove too powerful.

Through their own brand of "political" behavior, Garrisonians indicated that they were not unaware of the value of politics as an antislavery device. In November, 1841, Garrison heard that a small group of antislavery Whig Congressmen had decided, under Liberty man Joshua Leavitt's prodding, to carry on an intense campaign in Congress against slavery. Immediately *The Liberator* reminded the antislavery Whigs that they were "pledged in good faith not to flinch, or to yield one iota." And Garrison called upon their constituents to support them with antislavery petitions. If the voters remained "faithful to themselves," Garrison predicted, "their representatives will also be faithful."

When Congressman Joshua Giddings resigned after being censured in the House for his antislavery activity, Garrison and Stephen Foster, though they would not vote themselves, asked Giddings' constituents to return him "by an overwhelming (it ought to be unanimous) vote." In addition, Garrison attacked the pro-Southern wing of the Massachusetts Whig party in *The Liberator*, and he supported Congressional candidate John P. Hale, of New Hampshire, who tried to put together a coalition of Liberty men and dissident Whigs and Democrats to fight the annexation of Texas. Garrison also personally appeared at an anti-Texas meeting with Henry Wilson, later a Senator from Massachusetts.

Garrisonians used politics because they too understood that moral suasion alone was ineffective. Wendell Phillips said, "We expect to accomplish our object [abolition] long before the nation is converted into saints." But they warned abolitionists that spending time and energy in *direct* participation in third-party politics would take the edge off their radicalism, undermining their strength as agitators, and push them into compromises that would be destructive of their highest ideals. This, in some measure, is what happened to a great many political abolitionists.

As we have seen, some abolitionists in the late 1830's had tried to make abolitionism more respectable and thus more attractive by divorcing it from Garrison and so from other "ultra" ideas associated with him—e.g., women's rights and non-resistance. And in 1839 it appeared that the political abolitionists were attempting to force the Garrisonians out of the antislavery societies by setting up voting as a test for membership.

Lewis Tappan, at a meeting of the American Anti-Slavery Society in 1839, said, "If any abolitionists who possess the elective franchise have refused to *use* it to the best of their knowledge in behalf of the slave, it appears to us that they have . . . renounced the belief that slaves have a right to 'the protection of law.' " And James G. Birney, at a meeting of the Massachusetts Anti-Slavery Society in 1839, went so far as to proclaim it the duty of all abolitionists who had the right to vote to do so, and to suggest that those with religious scruples against voting ought to resign from the society.

The Garrisonians had no objection to political action so long as it remained a mode of agitation and did not require a compromise of principle. What they objected to was the attempt to embody antislavery sentiment in political measures before a supportive constituency had been built. Therefore, when anti-Garrisonians like Birney, Tappan, and Stanton forced a split in the American Anti-Slavery Society in 1840, they did so not to make political action possible but to dissociate themselves from radical Garrisonianism.

Furthermore, when the Liberty party was being formed, everyone seemed to agree that it should stand for just one idea—the abolition of slavery. James McCune Smith, a black physician and abolitionist from New York, expressed a widely held view when he said:

> There is but one way to attack Slavery through Political action: it is to make it the sole idea of that political action. All recognize the converse of this: all admit that the *one idea* of slavery has spread . . . into every institution in the land. . . . And if the one idea has

wrought this, how can we remove the results except by removing the one idea in its essence and in its mode?

The extremely small vote for presidential candidate James G. Birney in 1840 led some abolitionists, who apparently forgot that they weren't in the game to win, to question the one-idea approach. At a party convention in 1843, Gerrit Smith defended the one-idea platform by arguing that additional planks would adulterate the party; they would attract people whose commitment to abolitionism was not very strong. If this course were followed, Smith predicted, abolitionism would be submerged before long.

As late as 1845 the great majority of Liberty men favored the one-idea approach. But between 1843 and 1847 the tactic was widely questioned, and a remarkable collection of proposals and arguments for additional planks was put forward. Theodore Foster, editor of Michigan's leading abolitionist newspaper, *Signal of Liberty*, warned that Liberty men would sooner or later return to their traditional parties unless the Liberty platform made room for state and national issues other than slavery.

At the beginning of 1846, Birney argued publicly that the Liberty party could not expect to gain the support of most Northerners on the slavery issue alone. We are, he proclaimed, a *reform party* and must take a stand on all subjects, like tariffs and internal improvements, with which the voters (not only abolitionist voters) are deeply concerned.

And by 1847 Gerrit Smith and William Goodell agreed with Birney that the party should have a broad platform, and that it should be considered no longer a mere balance-of-power lobby but a permanent organization. In a few short years, these abolitionists had come a long way from the position that the Liberty party was a temporary vehicle of conversion! Most Liberty men, however, did not agree with the idea of broadening the platform. The result was the division of the political abolitionists into the one-idea Liberty party and the short-lived, broad-platform Liberty League.

The political abolitionists were more significantly divided in 1848 over the question of coalition with the newly emerged, less radical, and therefore more popular Free Soil party. Well before 1848, however, pressure to compromise had been applied to the abolitionists. As early as 1842, Salmon P. Chase of Ohio had urged that James G. Birney be replaced by a more moderate presidential candidate and that the party platform be toned down. In 1844, in what appeared to be a move away from its original radicalism, the Liberty party chose Thomas Morris, a staunch foe of black suffrage, as its vice-presidential candidate. There appeared to be a tacit recognition among some abolitionists that if political antislavery were to be successful at the polls, it would have to dissociate itself from the ideal of equality. And by the end of 1846 a significant number of Liberty party members were willing to accept leadership from men not of their original abolitionist persuasion.

John P. Hale, who was moderately antislavery but who refused to support either the abolition of slavery in the District of Columbia or the prohibition of the interstate slave trade, attracted the support of some Liberty men. Stanton and Leavitt, for example, thought Hale was with them "in heart and hand, in purpose and action." And by the early summer of 1847 antislavery newspapers from Maine to Illinois had come out in favor of a Liberty ticket headed by John P. Hale.

In a letter accepting the party's presidential nomination in 1848, Hale announced that should a broader-based antislavery coalition be formed, joining "the good and true of every party," he would step down and "enrol myself among the humblest privates who will rally under such a banner." And when in June, 1848, the Free Soil party, a coalition of disgruntled Democrats (Barnburners) led by Martin Van Buren and dissident Whigs, presented themselves as such a party, Liberty men were faced with a number of critical decisions. Should they, first of all, participate in the Free Soil convention in Buffalo?

Liberty men were troubled and disunited, but on one thing they were agreed: abolitionism's survival as a political issue demanded their attendance at Buffalo. Free Soilers were for non-extension of slavery. This was not abolitionism, but it was a step in the right direction, and it was popular. If Liberty men stayed away from the convention, they might be powerless to influence events. Their attendance, however, could provide the missing moral element for the Free Soil movement.

The political abolitionists were only reluctantly invited to the Free Soil convention. The Barnburners, the leading organizers of the Free Soil party, had a long history of Negrophobia and felt that Liberty men would only try to block their goal of nominating Martin Van Buren, who had made many proslavery, antiabolitionist statements in his career. They also wanted to write a general non-extensionist platform that could attract some abolitionist votes as well as the votes of whites who wanted to keep blacks out of the West. As one Barnburner put it:

> I speak not of the condition of the slave. I do not pretend to know, nor is it necessary that I should express an opinion in this place, whether the effect of slavery is beneficial or injurious to him. I am looking to its effects upon the white man, the free white man of . . . [the] territor[ies].

Liberty men, as the Barnburners had predicted, argued for John P. Hale's candidacy and for no platform concessions on the moral question of abolition or equal rights for blacks. Joshua Leavitt believed that the Liberty party could not support Martin Van Buren "without deliberately giving the lie to all our own declarations for fifteen years past." Van Buren, Leavitt said, is the "Northern man with Southern principles, not a hair changed."

The American and Foreign Anti-Slavery Society, made up mostly of political abolitionists, also came out against Martin Van Buren and platform concessions:

> Is it said, this is a "crisis"—a "special case"—"unite this once," and the Liberty party hereafter can act as efficiently as before? This is the stereotyped declaration on the eve of every Presidential election. . . . At every election temptations will be presented to postpone action on the great objects of your association, to carry some collateral issue, and thus friends or foes essay to make you instrumental in achieving inferior good at the expense of fundamental principles. . . . Never risk the success of the cause by making an issue on a minor point.

But when the Barnburners agreed to accept a platform calling for the limited goal of abolishing slavery in Washington, D.C., in addition to non-extension, Leavitt and Stanton were able to convince many Liberty men to go along with Van Buren's nomination. A remnant of Liberty men, including William Goodell, Gerrit Smith, and Lewis Tappan, unable to accept Van Buren and the dilution of the abolitionist ideal, maintained an independent radical Liberty party platform and ticket. They would continue to agitate through the 1850's.

Thus, by the fall of 1848, the Liberty party was virtually destroyed by fragmentation and cooptation. Its previous platforms had denounced the three-fifths and fugitive-slave clauses of the U. S. Constitution; they had focused on the moral wrong of slavery and had advocated equal rights for blacks. None of these planks was in the national Free Soil platform of 1848 endorsed by the majority of former Liberty men. And even after the anti-black Barnburners returned to the Democratic party, the national Free Soil party continued to avoid endorsing equal rights for blacks. Thus Liberty men who had joined with the Free Soil party had chosen to fight for the destruction of slavery without attempting to convert white men on the "Negro question." This represented a significant move away from moral suasion and a tacit assumption that abolition could be effected by political means alone.

The political abolitionists who remained outside the Free Soil party were also moving in the direction of coercion. They ultimately adopted the idea that the Constitution was an antislavery document. To abolish slavery, one need only insist that constitutional law be enforced. Goodell had written that the Constitution could not "secure *general liberty* . . . and at the same time guaranty *local slavery*. . . ." The direction of these abolitionists was away from moral suasion and toward political coercion of the South. For surely the South would not voluntarily accept an antislavery interpretation of the Constitution.

Yet the appearance of the Free Soil party was heartening to those abolitionists who continued to opt for moral suasion. Garrisonians had hoped that all voters would move in the direction of abolition, and Garrison thought that the nomination and election of antislavery candidates in traditionally conservative constituencies was "unmistakable proof of the progress we have made, under God, in changing public sentiment." Thus Garrison and his followers distinguished between old Liberty men— deserters from the cause of moral-suasion abolitionism—and newly awakened Free Soilers, whose moderately antislavery activities, Garrisonians optimistically believed, marked not a retreat from but an advance toward abolitionism.

Edmund Quincy, a Massachusetts Garrisonian, urged abolitionists to watch the progress of the Free Soil party with lively interest. He called on Garrisonians to act as informal campaign workers and try to make the electorate's "conscience uncomfortable." People desirous of relief will generally "seek it, in the first instance, in a Free Soil vote." In the last instance, it was hoped, people would embrace moral-suasion abolitionism.

Despite this involvement in politics, the Garrisonians, unlike the Liberty men, avoided formal political ties and thus the possibility of proslavery compromise. When the Republican party emerged as an even stronger antislavery coalition than the Free Soil party, Garrisonians saw it as "the legitimate product of moral agitation" but, again, most of them did not join. The Garrisonians thought it best to continue to agitate in the traditional way—moral suasion in the South, and castigation of politicians in the North—while at the same time offering encouragement to antislavery political movements. In 1859, for example, Garrison accused the Republican party of being a "timeserving, a temporizing, a cowardly party," but found hope in the fact that it possessed "materials for growth."

A few abolitionists felt that the South would not be convinced by either the Garrisonian or the political wing of the movement. These abolitionists began more and more to tolerate the idea of using violence to free the slaves.

The American Anti-Slavery Society had resolved in 1833 that abolitionists should never "countenance the oppressed in vindicating their rights by resorting to physical force," and that abolitionists themselves should never use physical force in their antislavery work. Some, like political abolitionist William Goodell, thought that if abolitionists used force, aggressively or defensively, the country would become "a scene of domestic violence in which the abolitionists would be almost certain to be overpowered." Other abolitionists, also convinced that violence would not work, emphasized other considerations. For example, nonresistant leader Adin Ballou, head of the Hopedale Community (an experiment in Christian socialism, and the first of the Utopian enterprises), and William Lloyd Garrison saw all coercion, and especially violence, as immoral. For them no use of force under any circumstances was acceptable.

The vast majority of abolitionists, however, were not nonresisters. Rather, they were moral suasionists who were committed to using nonviolence and "unresisting deportment" because these would win more friends for the cause. They thought forgiveness and sacrifice were more effective than coercion. They also thought forgiveness and sacrifice were more moral; but they generally did not mold such attitudes into a larger philosophical system. They were not necessarily opposed to violent self-defense under severe provocation, as when life and property were threatened, and they were not necessarily conscientious objectors to war.

Ultimately, frustration and weariness with the intransigence of American society would undermine, but by no means destroy, the commitment to nonviolence among moral suasionists and even among nonresisters. But during the 1830's and 1840's, abolitionists, in the face of physical attacks on their persons and their property, generally stayed true to nonviolence. Abolitionist meeting halls were burned in New York and Philadelphia; abolitionists' houses, including that of Lewis Tappan, were invaded and plundered; conventions were broken up by mobs; Theodore Dwight Weld was pelted with eggs and struck on the head with stones. William Lloyd Garrison estimated that between 1830 and 1850 there were three hundred cases of violent vigilante "reprisal" against those who espoused antislavery opinions. The abolitionists did not generally retaliate.

In 1835, Garrison himself was mobbed by "gentlemen of property and standing" during a Boston speech; and in the same year, abolitionist Amos Dresser, a Northern student attempting to raise money for his education by selling bibles in the South, was subjected to a kangaroo court in Nashville and whipped for peddling his wares wrapped in antislavery newspapers. Neither man resisted—not only because resistance was hardly possible under the circumstances, but as a conscious posture. In such instances, abolitionists reached a peak of awareness that they were responding to violence with nonviolence. Their behavior emphasized throughout the country the peaceable character of abolitionist work. James G. Birney, while defending abolitionists at a public debate in Ohio, called particular attention to their "peace principles." The black abolitionist professor William Allen told the Michigan Anti-Slavery Society a bit optimistically that peaceful agitation was "all the weapon we needed to give the death blow to the monster." The Pennsylvania Anti-Slavery Society in 1836 passed, by an overwhelming vote, a resolution strongly supporting nonviolence. In the following year, William Ladd, the evangelical founder of the American Peace Society, remarked that "every antislavery man is a peace man; or at least I have known but two or three exceptions."

But 1837 witnessed a small crisis in abolitionist ranks over the use of violence. In that year the abolitionist editor Elijah Lovejoy armed himself in order to defend his property and was shot to death. Lovejoy had been hounded out of the slave state of Missouri because of his antislavery opinions. He moved to Alton, in Illinois —a free state, where he hoped to be safe to write against slavery. Here, however, his printing presses were destroyed three times, his house was invaded, and his wife was brought to the verge of hysterical collapse. When a fourth new press arrived, Lovejoy determined that he would protect it. With the approval of the mayor of Alton, Lovejoy armed himself. When his press was attacked he raised his pistol but was quickly gunned down by one of the mob.

Abolitionists in the American Anti-Slavery Society and else-where were divided on whether or not to censure Lovejoy's action. Garrison acknowledged the right of self-defense under a secular, patriotic standard, but, he wrote in *The Liberator,* "In the name of Jesus of Nazareth who suffered himself to be unresistingly nailed to the Cross, we solemnly protest against any of his professed followers resorting to carnal weapons under any pretext or in any extremity whatever."

In the 1830's the influential Garrison was more emphatically nonresistant than ever, but he had no intention of making his own ideology a test for membership in the American Anti-Slavery Society. He did not ask the society to censure Lovejoy.

Lewis Tappan regretted Lovejoy's resort to physical force. But, he said, abolitionists, while pledged not to use "weapons of death to advance the cause," had not given away their right "to resist . . . assaults upon themselves or their property." In the end, the American Anti-Slavery Society did not condemn Lovejoy's attempt at violent self-defense. It was accepted by many moral-suasion abolitionists, at least tacitly, that nonviolence did not extend to self-defense. Yet it is important to note that throughout the Lovejoy controversy there was no thought of approving offensive violence of any kind by abolitionists, or of calling for slave insurrection. Indeed, the great majority of abolitionists were to remain generally nonviolent through 1861, and many maintained their "peace principles," actively or passively, even during the Civil War.

But from the very beginning of the militant abolitionist movement, in 1830, antislavery rhetoric contained an implicit call to violence. While the American Anti-Slavery Society explicitly denounced slave revolts as immoral from a Christian standpoint and impractical in the 1830's, most abolitionists, including Garrison, said that under secular standards slaves had a "right" to revolt. And many abolitionists, including nonresisters and Quakers, warned again and again that if the South did not free them, the slaves would eventually rise up and slaughter their oppressors. Consciously or otherwise, abolitionists often held out this veiled threat of violence in a futile attempt to prod slaveholders toward emancipation.

Furthermore, in the 1840's, abolitionists appeared to be more agreeable to the idea of slave revolts than they had been in the 1830's. When in 1841 an insurrection took place aboard the slaveship *Creole* on its way from Virginia to New Orleans, black abolitionist Frederick Douglass openly expressed pride in Madison Washington, who led the revolt and navigated the ship safely to British Bermuda. Only one white life was taken in the action, and the American and Foreign Anti-Slavery Society praised the bravery and humanity of the black slaves. And in

1843 a convention of blacks in Buffalo defeated by one vote a resolution advising slaves to seize their freedom and to defend it with violence if necessary.

Moreover, ever since the crisis engendered in 1837 by Lovejoy's death, the abolitionist position on nonviolence had been ambiguous. If violence was acceptable in extreme situations, as the abolitionists seemed to imply in 1837, could it be used to protect themselves and fugitives in the underground railroad? The question was not an abstract one, for by the 1840's the major abolitionist societies in the country endorsed aiding slaves to escape.

Quakers pioneered in underground-railroad efforts, and there was always a preference for peaceful methods in their work. But occasionally the success of nonviolent railroaders depended on the use of harassment, legal coercion, and even violence by others. And Frederick Douglass suggested that if a secret threat of violence hung over slave hunters, it would contribute to the success of the underground railroad.

The problem was intensified with the passage of a stronger Fugitive Slave Law in 1850. It seemed to abolitionists that the federal government had turned a deaf ear to twenty years of antislavery appeal. And to blacks, whether abolitionists, fugitives, or simple citizens, the law was frightening. In a period of fifteen months, 13,000 blacks, mostly free citizens of the North, fled to Canada.

In the face of this repressive situation, some abolitionists called for mass civil disobedience. The Rhode Island Anti-Slavery Society resolved that if it was not possible to hide fugitives or help them escape, "They shall be surrounded by a sufficiently numerous and influential Peace Committee to protect them from assault and capture." This approach to rescue work, though sometimes successful, ultimately involved much grappling and physical restraint. And in 1851, several rescues of fugitives from slave catchers succeeded only after a good deal of hand-to-hand fighting.

Frederick Douglass was ready to support, at least rhetorically, a much more violent method. "The only way to make the fugitive slave law a dead letter," he said, "is to make half a dozen or more dead kidnappers." Even Garrison encouraged those abolitionists who were not nonresisters to be faithful to their principles.

And sometimes there actually was bloodshed and death. In Pennsylvania in 1850, for example, a slave master on the hunt was killed by a group of escaped slaves wielding axes and guns. There was another killing in 1854, this time accidental, in an attempt by Boston abolitionists to prevent fugitive Anthony Burns from being returned to slavery. Boston, like many major cities in the North, had a vigilance committee made up of white and black abolitionists. Its task was to give legal aid to alleged fugitives and to help actual runaways in their flight. The committee was divided on how to proceed in the Burns case. The fugitive was already in the hands of law-enforcement officials, and the recently passed Fugitive Slave Law made it highly unlikely that Burns could be released legally. An impatient rump group split off from the vigilance committee, went to the courthouse, and battered down the door. In the process a guard was killed. The frightened group retreated without Burns, and the argument over means continued. It was soon settled when a large military force gathered in Boston. In the face of overwhelming strength, all the abolitionists agreed to be nonviolent.

Abolitionists had to face a difficult question: were they capable of developing forms of nonviolent action that could in fact protect fugitives? They took heart that the Burns case was not without positive repercussions. Boston citizens watching the drama played out became increasingly sympathetic to the plight of fugitive slaves. And no runaway was ever again returned from Massachusetts to slavery. Thus, although under terrible strain, abolitionists continued to believe that nonviolence was the best approach.

Theodore Parker wrote at the time of the Burns affair,

I deplore violence . . . let us do without it while we can, forever if we can. I am no nonresistant; yet I am glad the leading antislavery men are so—that, great as is the right of liberty, they would not shed a drop of blood to achieve it for all mankind; for though I think their doctrines extreme, they are yet nearer right, I think, than the common notions.

And J. Miller McKim, a Pennsylvania Garrisonian, claimed that by 1857, through court action, pressure on public officials, harassment, meetings, marches, and vigils, abolitionists had helped to develop enough public opposition to make the Fugitive Slave Law ineffective throughout the North.

Nonviolence faced new tests after 1854, when Congress repealed the Missouri Compromise, which had prohibited slavery north of the 36°30′ parallel, including the territories of Kansas and Nebraska. In 1855 and 1856 men who wished to make Kansas a free state competed for sovereignty in Kansas with men who wished to bring her into the union as a slave state. And there were sporadic instances of violence and death. So peaceful a woman as Angelina Grimké was moved to say, "We are compelled to choose between two evils, and all that we can do is take the *least*, and baptize liberty in blood, if it must be so." Some abolitionists even talked about supplying free-state men with rifles for self-defense. Garrison, upon discovering this possibility, wrote, "I think this is the time for radical peace men to renew their testimonies, dealing as tenderly as possible with settlers in Kansas (whose situation is undeniably a trying one), but repudiating a resort to carnal weapons as wrong *per se.*"

In 1856, Lawrence, the main town of the government free-state men had set up in the Territory of Kansas, was attacked and burned by proslavery forces bent on driving out the free-staters. John Brown, who was in Kansas at this time, took upon himself the role of avenging angel. With his four sons, his son-in-law, and a handful of others, he descended one night in May upon the sleeping community of Pottawottamie Creek, where he and his followers hacked five allegedly proslavery men to death. Then the Browns went into hiding and began a career of helping slaves escape.

Sympathetic historians such as Louis Ruchames see Brown's Kansas action as a kind of pre-emptive warfare aimed at defending Brown's free-state neighbors from future attack. But at the time of the massacre Brown's neighbors (although twenty years later dimmed memories would change some minds) were unanimous and unequivocal in their condemnation. And according to Stephen B. Oates, a recent biographer of Brown (1970), the

Pottawottamie Creek affair, instead of protecting people from future attack, initiated the most vicious period of guerrilla warfare on the frontier.

Yet some abolitionists who once had strong peace principles, like Theodore Parker and Gerrit Smith, were willing to back John Brown financially and subsequently joined the conspiracy that led to Brown's raid on the Harper's Ferry Arsenal in Virginia. It is likely that these abolitionists were misled, for Brown was capable of mendacity as well as fervent sincerity. In a letter to his wife shortly after Pottawottamie, Brown, in an apparent attempt to assert his innocence, reported that he had left the main body of armed free-staters with his "little company" and "encountered quite a number of proslavery men, and took quite a number prisoners. Our prisoners we let go; but we kept some four or five horses. We were immediately after this accused of murdering five men at Pottawottamie and great efforts have since been made to capture us." Brown asked his wife to send the letter to Gerrit Smith because he knew of "no other way to get these facts before the world." Brown was obviously willing to deceive, and perhaps some of the abolitionists were willing to be deceived. When Theodore Parker, for example, supplied money to Brown in 1859, he asked to be kept in ignorance of Brown's plans.

The tiny band of abolitionists who supported Brown's raid on Harper's Ferry in 1859 believed, as Brown claimed later, that he wished to seize the arsenal in order to open a front of guerrilla activity in the Virginia mountains and by this method to offer slaves an escape route to the North and ultimately Canada. The goal of helping a continuous stream of slaves escape into nearby mountains was risky, but conceivable. And the violence used in such an action could be seen as self-defensive. But many abolitionists saw Brown's scheme as a deliberate attempt to foment slave insurrection, which could lead to failure and would inevitably involve random and offensive violence. Frederick Douglass, for example, contended afterward that Brown had made the gallows as glorious as the cross. But the black abolitionist leader had specifically refused to aid Brown in his Harper's Ferry conspiracy. For Brown had intimated to Douglass that insurrection was indeed part of his plan. "When I strike," Brown had said, "the bees will begin to swarm, and I shall want you to help me hive them." Garrison, again using his logical double standard, ranked Brown with the heroes of Bunker Hill. He went so far as to suggest that cowardice was as wrong as violence and that to do violence to overcome injustice was better than to continue to be cowardly and servile. And the non-resistant Henry C. Wright said, "Resistance to slaveholders and slavehunters is obedience to God, and a sacred duty to man. . . . [It is our] right and duty . . . to instigate the slaves to insurrection."

John Brown was valuable to the cause in that his eloquence and dignity in the face of execution won much public sympathy. His martyrdom tended, as martyrdom generally does, to unite and intensify the commitment and militancy of the crusaders. But the tradition of nonviolence was very strong. When the South seceded in the winter of 1860–61, some abolitionists, including Stephen Foster and William Goodell, did suggest the use of violence by the North, believing that abolitionists had "no moral or political right to allow [the slaves] to be kidnapped out of the Union, when it is the religious and constitutional duty of the Union to set them free." But most abolitionists, from all wings of the movement, were in favor of letting the South and its slaveholders secede peacefully.

Here, in one sense, was the fulfillment of the disunion idea for which some abolitionists had been agitating for twenty years. Disunion, it was now argued, would not only isolate the South and hold up its peculiar institution to the moral condemnation of the world; the actual political separation would also remove the protection of the U. S. Army from slavery and thus allow slave rebellions more possibility of success. The South would therefore be *forced* to give up slavery. This point, which had only been implied in the earlier disunion agitation, was now made openly. Wendell Phillips asked:

What supports slavery? Northern bayonets, calming the masters' fear. . . . Disunion leaves God's natural laws to work their good results. . . . Under God's law, insurrection is the tyrant's check. Let

us stand out of the path, and allow the Divine law to have free
course.

Thus violence was implicit in the abolitionists' disunion solution for the crisis of 1860–61. Still, the abolitionists did not want
war. They did not even want a slave rebellion. What these weary
men hoped for was voluntary emancipation by the masters,
perhaps out of fear of slave rebellion.

When war finally came, however, many who had been unwilling to support such offensive violence as John Brown's at
Harper's Ferry *were* ready to join battle if the Civil War were
made a war for black freedom. The central task of the abolitionists in the early years of the war was to make emancipation
an explicit aim of the war. Once that was accomplished, abolitionists would dedicate themselves to the struggle for racial
equality.

6. The Black Abolitionists

Our elevation as a race is almost wholly dependent upon our own exertions. . . . *The history of other oppressed nations will confirm us in this assertion . . . the oppressed nation itself has always taken a prominent part in the conflict.* —Frederick Douglass, 1855

In her biography of black abolitionist Charles B. Ray, Mrs. Ray contested the view that boldness in the cause of abolitionism was to be expected of a black man. Exclusion, disenfranchisement, and general oppression made the mass of blacks dependent in one way or another upon whites, and therefore, she explained, free blacks required extraordinary qualities to espouse openly the cause of the enslaved or to identify overtly with the movement to improve their own plight.

Despite this dependence, which forced many blacks to adopt a manner of indifference as a kind of survival insurance, blacks constituted a relatively high proportion of abolitionist leadership in antebellum America. In New York State, for example, where blacks accounted for less than two per cent of the general population between 1830 and 1860, nine of the state's fifty most important abolitionist leaders were black. Three of the first four sales agents of *The Liberator* were black. James Forten, a wealthy black sailmaker from Philadelphia, made up the finan-

cial losses of the paper for a good while, and free blacks constituted the majority of subscribers in the early years.

Widespread black commitment to liberation is further indicated by the large numbers of free urban blacks who were
attracted to the National Negro Convention Movement between
1830 and 1835. This movement was generally concerned with
repeal of the "black laws" of various Northern states, the
advancement of the free black, and the abolition of slavery. It
was also an early manifestation of the recognition by blacks
of the need for racial solidarity and collective action independent of whites. After 1840 there was an even stronger abolitionist emphasis in the Convention movement, and by the 1850's
there was scarcely a black state or national convention that failed
to denounce slavery or to demand equality for blacks before the
law.

Blacks held antislavery meetings between 1832 and 1834 in at
least twenty-three cities in at least ten states. And between 1834
and 1838, blacks formed their own antislavery societies in
Rochester, Newark, Nantucket, Lexington, Troy (Michigan),
New York, and Philadelphia.

The founding of these societies did not prevent blacks from
contributing their talents to the integrated abolitionist associa-
tions. The New England Anti-Slavery Society continued to have
substantial numbers of blacks in its ranks. The society, founded
on January 1, 1832, in a classroom of the African Baptist Church
in Boston's black section, was one of the first to advocate immediate abolition. Eighteen of the original seventy-two members
were black. In 1834, ten members of the Board of Managers and
three of the twelve members of the executive committee of the
American Anti-Slavery Society were blacks.

The Vigilance Committees, organized to aid fugitives, had a
predominantly black membership. In Philadelphia, New York,
and Boston, some of the committees were integrated and some
were composed only of blacks. In Cleveland and Detroit, the
vigilance groups were all black.

While the extent of the operations of the underground railroad has been exaggerated, it probably helped some 50,000
slaves to escape between 1830 and 1860, and blacks frequently
contributed to this effort. Great numbers of those who did

abolitionist work in the South were blacks—for example, Harriet Tubman, herself an escapee from slavery, made some fifteen expeditions into slave territory and brought back more than two hundred fugitives. Despite immense obstacles, the "oppressed nation itself ... played a prominent part in the conflict," as Frederick Douglass said.

Some of the special qualities necessary for the reform roles of the black abolitionists appear to have been engendered by theological training, for the ministry was by far the most common occupation of the black leaders in the abolitionist movement. These black abolitionists were educated for the ministry in an era when Protestantism emphasized the sufficiency of human reason in matters of religion, as well as the idea that God's goal was the perfection and happiness of all his children. Therefore slavery was seen by them as blatant sin.

Approximately 30 per cent of the blacks who sat on the original boards of the American Anti-Slavery Society, the Middletown (Connecticut) Anti-Slavery Society, and the Pennsylvania Anti-Slavery Society were clergymen. The majority of black abolitionists in New York State were ministers. And the eight blacks among the founders of the American and Foreign Anti-Slavery Society in May 1840—including editor Samuel Cornish—were all clergymen educated in the context of Protestant perfectionism.

In nineteenth-century America, black leadership generally came from ministerial ranks, for most other professions were virtually closed to blacks. But few black ministers were trained in theology, nor did most of them publicly advocate abolition. Thus the large proportion of black abolitionists who had been at one time or another educated for the ministry suggests that perfectionist theological training was significant in predisposing blacks toward abolitionism. Most of those abolitionists who were not clergymen were nevertheless actively and intensely religious. Their thinking was rooted in the principles of evangelical, perfectionist Christianity, a Christianity that was moving away from the concept of original sin (often used to justify slavery in the past) to the idea of sin as the inhibiting and repressive temporal force blocking the path to the millennium.

Black leaders were aware of the relationship between their

religious intensity and their abolitionist orientation, and they articulated it consistently. Charles B. Ray, pastor of the Bethesda Congregational Church in New York for more than twenty years, said in relation to his seemingly inexhaustible labors in the abolitionist field that he had "no disposition to sit idly by when there is so much Christian work within reach and pressing upon one's hands to do." Slavery and discrimination were, after all, violations of the ancient Christian ideals of brotherhood and love, as well as inconsistent with the values of liberty and equality more recently emphasized by Christians and equally central to contemporary secular thought.

Another Congregational minister, Samuel Ringgold Ward, born of slave parents who later carried him as a child to freedom, preached that slavery was in reality the buying and selling of the image of God. Between 1840 and 1850, Ward lectured in nearly every church, auditorium, and schoolhouse in western and central New York. He reminded religious men and ministers, many of whom relied on older Christian tenets in defense of slavery, that since blacks were men, equal in the eyes of God to other men, slavery was adultery, fornication, and incest. Could He who gave the law from Sinai approve such an institution? Ward asked rhetorically. But Ward's aim, like that of many of his associates, seemed to be not so much to preach the gospel of heaven as to preach a worldly gospel, so that Americans choosing to be called Christians might learn to live up to their own lofty professions and respect the dignity and rights of fellow humans.

Black abolitionist leaders, religiously motivated like their white colleagues, were moved to condemn existing churches and were finally impelled to establish religious institutions of their own— which suggests that while religious philosophy may have operated as a radicalizing force, the institution of the church itself was conservative. The black church existed long before the abolitionist movement, and black churches in general continued throughout the years of crisis to be merely perfunctory in their abolitionism. But churches established by blacks with abolitionist sentiments generally served as stations on the underground railroad, and their ministers promoted a social gospel that stressed the church militant in a fellowship of concern. The existence of black churches created another problem for the integration-minded abolitionists, but the independence of these churches allowed those so inclined to speak out without fear of offending a Southern wing. And white abolitionists frequently attended black churches.

In addition to religious intensity, the black abolitionists as a group had achieved a relatively high level of education. Many were tutored in the schools that were supported by black abolitionists and antislavery societies until they were incorporated as public schools in city and state systems. And in an era when such institutions as Columbia, Brown, and Wesleyan refused admission to blacks or, as an abolitionist put it, "encouraged a prejudice which created an atmosphere in which a colored student could not live," the ranks of the black abolitionists were remarkably well filled with college-educated men, graduated from the University of Glasgow, Princeton, Oxford, Oberlin, the University of Vermont, and Oneida Institute, among other schools. George B. Vashon, Charles L. Reason, and William G. Allen, who were among these college graduates, went on to become college professors themselves.

It is possible that education, like theological orientation, made these blacks more aware of the destructiveness of what Samuel Ringgold Ward described as white "Negro-hate," that force that "discourages [the black person's] efforts, damps his ardor, blasts his hopes, and embitters his spirits." It is possible that education enabled these men to see the intimate relationship between the continued existence of the institution of slavery and their own demoralized position as blacks in white America; it is possible that this recognition led to their rudimentary black-nationalist conception that no black is free until all blacks are free. And it is possible that their education and their demonstrated ability gave them the self-confidence necessary to speak out on these matters.

Isolating the motivation of the black abolitionist is a difficult if not impossible task, and the foregoing remarks are only imprecise impressions. One must also look beyond the level of education and religious affiliation to ponder the existential experience of being black in a racist country whose core society is white, of being a man whose status in the minds of his countrymen is at best ambivalent, and what this does to individuals of differing sensitivity, perceptiveness, and strength of character.

One must also take into account specific personal experience —for example, that of the Reverend Theodore S. Wright, whose father, R. P. G. Wright, advocated direct action from the earliest period of the struggle against slavery. What effect did the model supplied by the father have on the son? Henry Highland Garnet was a slave for the first nine years of his life; what effect did this have on his abolitionist motivation and militancy? What effect did the dangerous flight from oppression have on those fugitive slaves who later served in and often led the abolitionist movement?

Espousal of abolitionist sentiment by whites, especially after 1830, when the movement against slavery became more strident and radical, no doubt acted as a stimulus to blacks, calling forth hitherto underused energies and powers. But it is important to keep in mind that black militancy preceded William Lloyd Garrison's abolitionist activities. As early as 1827, *Freedom's Journal,* co-edited by Samuel E. Cornish, consistently supplied clear evidence that there were free blacks who were strongly dissatisfied with slavery and colonization, as well as with racial prejudice and its effects. In 1829, David Walker, a self-taught black man, deeply swayed by religious feeling and very active in the abolitionist movement, issued a seventy-six-page pamphlet which the Quaker Benjamin Lundy described as the most inflammatory publication in history. Found circulating among blacks in Savannah, Georgia, and later in the upper South, *David Walker's Appeal,* directly advising slaves to use violence to free themselves, frightened two states into enacting laws forbidding the circulation of written materials of "incendiary nature" and the teaching of slaves to read or write. And as early as January, 1817, only days after the establishment of the American Colonization Society, free blacks of Virginia held a meeting to protest the society's plan to export blacks to Africa. In August of the same year, "the largest meeting ever yet held by the colored people of the free states" took place in Philadelphia. More than three thousand black people met and unanimously endorsed a statement by James Forten explaining black hostility toward colonization and denouncing the policy of expatriation as "little more merciful than death."

Organized protest all over the country continued for years, but it would take militant blacks, like Theodore S. Wright and Samuel Cornish, who were for emancipation without expatriation, to arouse white churchmen and abolitionists. It took black rage and black leadership to win white antislavery people away from the American Colonization Society, which so many had supported in the belief that it was their Christian duty to do so. Lewis Tappan believed that it was the black leaders' "united and strenuous opposition to the expatriation scheme that first induced Garrison and others to oppose it." And the entire second half of Garrison's *Thoughts on African Colonization* (1832) was devoted to demonstrating and explaining black hostility toward emigration to Liberia.

Some blacks in this period did see emigration as a possible solution to the American dilemma. Paul Cuffe, a black New Bedford shipowner, in 1815 took thirty-eight free blacks to Sierra Leone at his own expense. By 1816 Cuffe reported that so many applications for emigration came across his desk "he might have colonized the greater part of Boston and vicinity." Moreover, there were scores of migrants to Liberia, and several articulate spokesmen for the emigrationist position—including John B. Russwurm, co-editor of *Freedom's Journal*, a newspaper he founded in 1827 because "too long have others spoken for [blacks]." On the whole, however, there developed an incipient group consciousness rather than a drive for rigid separatism, a call for collective action to achieve equality within the United States rather than an advocacy of departure.

Black militancy not only preceded white militancy but it consistently gave abolitionism its hard edge and made it much more effective than it could otherwise have been. This was a function not only of the breadth and intensity of black involvement in the abolitionist movement but also of the injection of a black perspective on the issues.

Black abolitionists were effective in creating a good deal of white sympathy for the crusade as well as in ensuring that abolitionism did not become merely antislavery—i.e., in ensuring that the movement continued to embrace a vision of a society based on racial justice as well as the goal of legal emancipation. The black's effectiveness in arousing white sympathy is due in part to the kind of apologetics surrounding the peculiar institution. The rationalization for slavery rested upon two basic lies. First, proslavery men asserted, especially after 1830, that the system was a benevolent patriarchy, eliciting gratitude and general contentment from its laboring population. Second, it was affirmed that in any case the enslaved people were innately inferior to the masters; that their situation therefore represented simply a practical accommodation predetermined by natural and supernatural forces. These deceits could be, and were, most effectively unmasked only by blacks themselves.

The fugitive played an especially important role here, for, as Angelina Grimké wrote to her future husband, Theodore Dwight Weld, in 1838, "Many and many a tale of romantic horror can the slaves tell." They could and did transmit to white people far removed from the environment of the peculiar institution the atmosphere of bloodhounds, chains, whips, and dungeons, and "the pulse of the four millions of slaves and their desire for freedom." Fugitives who participated in the abolitionist movement worked successfully at erasing the notion that the black slave was happy. And the ability displayed in the writing, oratory, and organizational work of William Wells Brown, Lewis and Milton Clarke, Henry Bibb, Frederick Douglass, and others went far toward undermining the belief in black inferiority. This effect was reinforced by the abolitionist work of other able blacks who were not fugitives—for example, Paul Cuffe, merchant and shipbuilder, William Whipper, a highly successful lumber dealer, and James McCune Smith, a New York physician.

Many fugitives published accounts of their escapes and the beginning of their new lives as free men. These works were emotionally appealing and exciting and made slavery more real and more evil to substantial numbers of readers. Many of the works like Douglass' *Narrative of My Life* (1845), went through several editions and versions. Solomon Northup's *Twelve Years a*

Slave alone had a circulation of at least 27,000. Fugitives frequently spoke at abolitionist meetings as well. Somehow, people who paid little heed to the warnings and declarations of white abolitionists were willing to listen to William Wells Brown when he told of "slavery as it is, and its influence upon the morals and character of the American people."

Larry Gara, a modern student of fugitive participation in the abolitionist movement, maintains that even proslavery people in the North were moved by the fugitives' plight. Apparently seeing the fugitive made slavery real, harder to deny. Light mulatto fugitive slaves were especially disconcerting to white audiences. After hearing Ellen Craft, a fugitive mulatto, speak in Boston in 1849, Massachusetts abolitionist Samuel J. May said:

> To think of such a woman being held as a piece of property subject to be traded off to the highest bidder (while it is in reality no worse or wickeder than when done to the blackest woman that ever was) does yet stir a community brought up in prejudice against color a thousand times more deeply than could be effected in similar circumstances.

Fugitives also played the important role of relating slavery to other issues that could arouse large numbers of Northerners. It was only when slavery became associated with civil liberties and sectional pride that the tiny abolitionist movement which was interested in increasing the freedom of blacks grew into the larger antislavery movement which was interested in reducing the political power and prestige of Southern slaveholders. Incidents involving fugitives often provided the link. The escapee was after all the sympathetic center of the exciting drama of man in distress. And the arbitrary enforcement of the Fugitive Slave Laws of 1793 and 1850, in combination with the arrest and prosecution of abolitionists who violated the laws, converted many people to an antislavery position, if only on the peripheral questions of civil liberties and sectional pride.

Manifestations of the conversion appeared in some Northern states in the 1840's in the form of "personal liberty laws" which forbade state officials from taking part in the enforcement of the federal laws for the return of fugitive slaves. And by 1854 popular sentiment against the Fugitive Slave Law was so strong that the federal government spent $40,000 in order to return only one fugitive—Anthony Burns—and used twenty-two companies of state militia, four platoons of marines, a battalion of U. S. artillerymen, and Boston's entire police force. Observing all this, Theodore Parker commented angrily, "A few years ago they used to tell us, 'Slavery is an abstraction, we at the North have nothing to do with it!' " And Bronson Alcott remarked, "The question 'What has the North to do with slavery?' is visibly answered." The Massachusetts officials cooperating in Burns's recapture were retired from public life at the next election.

Fugitive slaves, in addition to eliciting widespread white sympathy, imbued the abolitionists with fresh vigor and determination. The small but steady influx of new arrivals dramatically and incessantly made the evil of slavery more personal for the abolitionists, white and black. Black abolitionists, former slaves or not, served by their presence, their activity, and their critical perspective as an educational force within the movement, making white abolitionists aware of and ultimately willing to transcend their relative conservatism on the issue of racial integration.

In 1834, the American Anti-Slavery Society announced that it favored neither social mixing of the two races nor the admittance of blacks to civil rights in the white society beyond what their "intellectual and moral worth" made advisable. And Theodore S. Wright told the black and white delegates to the New York State Anti-Slavery Society Convention in Utica in 1837, "Prejudice must be killed or slavery will never be abolished. . . . Abolitionists must annihilate in their own bosoms the cord of caste." Samuel Cornish agreed; he wrote that unless abolitionists "should judge of us as they do of other men . . . they never can succede [sic]." Too many white abolitionists, Samuel Ringgold Ward regretted, "best loved the colored man at a distance."

Black abolitionists believed that the prejudice of their white counterparts was reflected in their halfheartedness in carrying out one of their announced purposes—the elevation of the free black. "When they come to the grand doctrine to destroy the very spirit of slavery," said Ward, "there they are defective. Their doctrine is to set the slave free and let him take care of himself."

White abolitionists sincerely desired and were working for true black equality after emancipation, and the Liberty party devoted much of its time to the "black problem" in the North. But many abolitionists never outgrew a paternalistic racism; their efforts for integration were most often abortive and were not generally undertaken in the important area of economic equality. Abolitionist organizations made some token efforts to help the black workingmen, and some wealthy individuals such as Gerrit Smith developed well-meaning programs involving relocation and education; but in general, the picture is one of inadequacy. Blacks were aware of this. When the *Colored American*, for example, reviewed the economic plight of the black man in the wake of the national economic crisis of 1837, it noted that not one local abolitionist had placed a black man in any conspicuous position in his business establishment.

Blacks had sorrowfully learned that many white abolitionists, including their beloved Garrison, had a tendency to emphasize long-range, abstract goals. Blacks therefore came to see their task as ensuring that the abolitionists never forgot the immediate practical needs of the persecuted "free people of color." If the goal of abolitionism was to teach the white community that a society based on racial justice and brotherly love was feasible, white abolitionists would have to eliminate the cord of caste from their own bosoms and be consistent with their stated beliefs. White abolitionists would have to be pushed to "lay the ax right down at the root of the tree."

Some blacks thought they might be more effective in these efforts by setting up their own organizations dedicated to self-help and direct nonviolent action. Feelings on this question came to a head in 1840 with the schism in abolitionist ranks between the Garrisonian moral suasionists and those abolitionists who wanted to move the slavery issue more directly into politics. The activist blacks of the Philadelphia and New York areas competed in the late 1830's and early 1840's for control of black abolitionism. The Philadelphians, led by William Whipper and Robert Purvis, leaned more toward the nonresistance of Garrison, and they were less inclined to work through separatist black organizations. The New York blacks, led by the ministers Theodore Wright, Charles Ray, and Samuel Cornish, were more willing to affiliate with abolitionist political parties, and while they participated in integrated abolitionist organizations, they also worked through separatist all-black groups.

Few blacks rejected out of hand any cooperation with whites, but by the 1840's many were ready for all-black action that was supportive and supplemental as well as distinctive. "If we act with our white friends," thought Charles B. Ray, "the words we utter will be considered theirs, or their echo." Another black leader believed that "to talk about waiting till our friends get right is nonsense. We must act for ourselves." At least one activist black New Yorker, James McCune Smith, disagreed, believing that separate action was a virtual acknowledgment that there are rights peculiar to skin color.

When some of the white abolitionist papers claimed that separate black conventions perpetuated the idea of segregation, the *Colored American* reaffirmed its support of independent action. The wrongs inflicted on blacks, argued Samuel Ward, made black meetings and organization indispensable; his white friends would have understood this, he thought, had they "worn a colored skin from October '17 to June '40, as I have in this pseudo-republic."

In the 1840's separatism recommended itself to more and more black abolitionists. For after ten years of militant abolitionism, slavery seemed as securely entrenched as ever, and the condition of the free black person remained substantially unchanged. Indeed, in some places it had sharply deteriorated. Many black activists increasingly encouraged varieties of nascent black nationalism, ranging from the minimal form—racial solidarity as a stepping stone to integration—to, by the 1850's, the ultimate form—emigration. Just as recent black nationalism can be seen, at least in part, as a response to the aftermath of the 1960's civil rights "victories" that did not bring any visible improvement to black masses, nineteenth-century "black nationalism" can be seen as a response to the apparent failure of the abolitionist movement.

Group consciousness among blacks developed not only in response to white exclusiveness, and not only as a vehicle for integration, but in recognition and affirmation of the cultural heritage of black Americans, and as an attempt at mental "decolonization." Even Frederick Douglass, the most consistent of the integrationists, reflected some of this latter position. He certainly emphasized racial cooperation and unity as the means for blacks to gain the respect of whites, counteract prejudice, and ease the way toward recognition of their manhood and citizenship. However, Douglass advocated unity among blacks, not only for the purpose of protest and agitation over slavery and citizenship rights; he recognized the need for racial solidarity in economic development of black communities and in development of a source of psychological sustenance as well.

In any case, by 1850, most black abolitionists operated on the assumption that emancipation and the advancement of the free black were sides of the same coin, and that collective action independent of whites was essential. The revived Negro National Convention, meeting in Philadelphia in 1853, made the point when it resolved: "In *our* elevation lies the freedom of our enslaved brethren; in that elevation is centered the germ of our own high destiny, and the best well-being of the whole people." The convention sought to tighten the bonds of racial unity by creating a National Council to supervise highly organized efforts toward black advancement.

Still, most black efforts in this direction—including the integrationist American Moral Reform Society and the black-nationalist Cooperative Movement (a practical effort to root social freedom in economic power)—exploited the basic values of American culture. If white American society valued self-help, independence, virtuous character, the accumulation of property, and national pride, then these attributes, it was thought, would also be an aid to blacks in their struggle for advancement. Most black activists astutely fashioned major American ideologies into a program that would elevate an oppressed group and secure its inclusion in the larger society.

The great majority of black abolitionists, unlike Booker T. Washington after them, were unwilling to accept second-class citizenship and were always clear and explicit about their desire for full equality. Furthermore, few, if any, of the activist blacks believed, with Horace Greeley, that the cultivation of "good character" and industriousness and the acquisition of as much property as possible were substitutes for protest, agitation, and direct nonviolent action in the quest for first-class citizenship.

For many years, blacks tried railroad ride-ins in places that segregated their transportation systems, such as New York and Philadelphia; pray-ins at churches where blacks were barred or kept in subordinate positions; boycotting of schools where there were segregated systems, as in Boston; and various forms of noncooperation with the government, such as tax resistance. Charles Lenox Remond, writing from England, where he was lecturing, urged blacks to be more radical in their demands, adding: "Let every colored man, called upon to pay taxes to any institution in which he is deprived or denied its privileges and advantages, withhhold his taxes, although it costs imprisonment or confiscation. Let our motto be—no privileges, no pay."

These quasi-coercive actions were in some measure a rejection of moral suasion. But they were never institutionalized or organized on a mass scale. Many black as well as white abolitionists believed that change by coercion could never be fundamental or permanent. They doubted that coercion could touch their opponents' consciences.

Samuel Cornish hinted at the possibility of using direct nonviolent action as a form of controlled coercion. He said in 1838, "The strong arm of coercion of some kind is needed to awaken . . . [proslavery advocates] to duty." And when David Ruggles said in 1840, "We of the North are slaves to the community, and ever will be until we rise, and by the help of Him who governs the destiny of nations, go forward, and like the reformed inebriates, ourselves strike for reform—individual, general, and radical reform, in every ramification of society," he seemed to be advocating the more impatient forms of nonviolence on a mass scale. But because direct action was not organized enough nor sufficiently incorporated into a theory of nonviolence (as Martin

Luther King would do later), few became aware of its power.

Thus when blacks became frustrated by the entrenched position of those whites who believed they gained from slavery and racial discrimination, when they were disappointed by the failure of "moral suasion" to secure the freedom of those in bondage or to elevate the free black, when they were denied suffrage, when they saw a more repressive Fugitive Slave Law enacted, and when they saw a nation readying itself continually to sacrifice the rights of blacks to the prospect of sectional reconciliation, they increasingly moved away from Garrisonian moral suasion and into more political activity. Concomitantly they assumed a more politically militant, if not more ideologically radical, posture.

Modern historians Benjamin Quarles, Charles Harris Wesley, and Howard Bell agree that the great majority of black leaders came strongly to favor the use of political power to strike at slavery and elevate the free black. "Political power is a mighty Anti-Slavery engine," said the *Colored American* in 1839; "We hold that all true abolitionists should go to the polls and vote." Once politics was recognized as necessary and legitimate, abolition of suffrage restrictions in the "free states" became a key issue in the black activist crusade. For as late as 1860, equal suffrage existed only in New England, excluding Connecticut. In the remaining states blacks were barred from the polls or faced with a property requirement.

The Liberty party, organized in 1840, won the enthusiastic backing of the *Colored American*, and black abolitionists including Henry Highland Garnet, William C. Munro, Theodore S. Wright, Henry Bibb, David Lewis, and Charles B. Ray took the field to drum up support for the party. The Buffalo convention of the Liberty party in 1843 marked the first time that American blacks were included in the leadership of a political convention.

Frederick Douglass, Charles Lenox Remond, and William Nell, still hopeful that moral suasion could be effective, were opposed to Liberty party affiliation at this time. But black abolitionists suffered a less severe break over this issue than their white counterparts had done. For blacks, whether moral suasionists or ballot-minded Liberty party adherents, shared more deeply the primary goal of black advancement. By 1847 powerful moral suasionists like William Nell were cooperating in abolitionist political activity with the militant Garnet and the impatient Charles B. Ray. Even Charles Remond and Frederick Douglass were side by side with Henry Bibb and Samuel R. Ward at the Free Soil party convention in 1848.

Black leaders of all persuasions understandably had mixed feelings about supporting the Free Soil party. On the one hand, in Ohio the party championed black suffrage, and in Massachusetts Free Soil men successfully battled to remove discrimination in marriage laws, transportation, and public schools. On the other hand, the national Free Soil party was led by disaffected, politically motivated New York Democrats whose record on black rights was anything but praiseworthy. Samuel R. Ward took a strong stand against the party and its nominee, Martin Van Buren, and entreated people to "vote for Gerrit Smith and Equal Rights." The majority of enfranchised blacks apparently took a half-a-loaf attitude, believing it wiser to support the Free Soil party because it had a chance to win.

Yet despite black support, the Free Soil party platform ultimately stood for containment rather than extermination of slavery and was totally silent as to discrimination against free blacks. In 1854, the Reverend J. W. Loguen said that his brethren should "strike the blow for themselves, and not wait for the hairsplitting of politicians and speakers."

Despite the black abolitionists' disappointment with the performance of politicians, politics continued to have great appeal for most of them. This may have had something to do with previous deprivation as well as with the fact that politics was an all-consuming American activity. The dialectic of political participation itself leads men involved in it, white or black, to hope that the apparent power bottled up in the system can be released to effect particular ends. Thus, even though the emerging Republican party made no special effort to attract black voters, and despite the fact that part of the party's appeal was its racist notion of "saving the west for the Caucasians," several black leaders hailed this new and stronger party committed to the containment of slavery. And many blacks supported the Republicans as the lesser of the evils.

The actions of Frederick Douglass are indicative of the frustration and ambivalence of the black abolitionist as he faced his political choices. In 1855, Douglass, along with black clergymen J. W. Loguen and Amos G. Beman, joined Gerrit Smith in the Radical Abolition party, refusing fellowship with the Republicans. By 1856, however, Douglass was supporting the Republican party. Between 1856 and 1860, as the Republicans moved from the zenith of their antislavery appeal, giving up antislavery altogether in some areas, and increasingly emphasizing more attractive issues, Douglass once more cut his affiliation with them. Early in 1860, Douglass believed that 10,000 votes for Gerrit Smith would do more for the abolition of slavery than 2,000,000 for Lincoln, "or any man who stands pledged before the world against all interference with slavery in the slave states and who is not opposed to making free states a hunting ground for men under the Fugitive Slave Law." Yet, and here again one is in awe of the ability of politics to arouse hope in those with little power, Douglass ended by campaigning for Lincoln.

In 1855, several New York blacks, increasingly aware of the need for separate black action, organized the New York State Suffrage Association as a black balance-of-power party. But no solution for blacks was to come for the political arena at least through 1863. Tightly united Southern power blocs, in combination with Northern politicians fearful of sectional discord, repealed the Missouri Compromise, which had for over thirty years prohibited slavery north and northwest of the 36°30′ parallel; Democratic presidents misused their power to "make Kansas sure for slavery" in order to placate the ever-demanding Southern wing of the party; Republican candidates ignored the slavery question when it was not a vote-getting issue and appealed to Negrophobia where that was popular.

It is no wonder that black militancy increased to the point that black abolitionists openly hailed as a hero John Brown, the abolitionist who staged an armed but unsuccessful slave-rescue mission in Virginia. The toleration of violence in the cause of liberation was not a sudden development as far as blacks were concerned. David Walker's *Appeal,* directing slaves in 1829 to emancipate themselves through violent means if necessary, has already been mentioned. Samuel Cornish, at the time of Elijah

Lovejoy's martyrdom in 1837, said, "We honestly confess that we have yet to learn what virtue there would be in using moral weapons . . . against a kidnapper or a midnight incendiary with a lighted torch in his hand." He even believed that "offensive aggression" could be "indispensable to personal liberty and rights."

At the 1843 Buffalo Convention of the Free People of Color, Henry Highland Garnet said that "voluntary submission" to slavery was sinful. "It is your solemn and imperative duty to use every means . . . moral, intellectual, and physical, that promises success" in attaining freedom. Garnet advised slaves to cease toiling for the tyrants—"If they then commence the work of death, they and not you will be responsible for the consequences." A resolution that the convention support the sentiment that "There is not much hope of redemption without the shedding of blood" failed of passage by the slim margin of 19–18. The abolitionist lecturer Charles Lenox Remond and Frederick Douglass, in attendance at Buffalo, spoke for "trying the moral means a little longer"; others with nonresistant principles, including William Nell, Robert Purvis, and William Whipper, strongly opposed Garnet.

The majority of black leaders thus narrowly affirmed a nonviolent position, but few of them were nonresistance men. Therefore, further frustration and disappointment stemming from the continued victories of the slave interests and from the intransigent refusal of a racist society to recognize what was just would push the black abolitionists in more militant directions.

Those blacks who led in vigilance committees, for example, were abolitionists dedicated to some degree of nonviolence, but in their attempts to protect runaway slaves they often found their nonviolence under strain. The Garrisonian Charles L. Remond came to favor using some forms of defensive violence. And even Robert Purvis, who had said in 1836 that blacks did not desire to achieve their rights by "blood and carnage," a few years later gave a fugitive a gun to fend off slave catchers who had invaded the Purvis estate.

In 1848, a Boston meeting of blacks recognized the validity of violent self-defense against a return to bondage even if it meant bloodshed. A year later, black abolitionists in Maine and New Hampshire seriously debated their obligation to give physical aid to slave insurrection. Ohio's black abolitionists, who had six years earlier opposed Henry Highland Garnet at Buffalo for fear of retaliation by white mobs at home, in 1849 proposed resolutions encouraging slaves to escape and citizens to trample under foot any law that "conflicts with reason, liberty and justice, either North or South," and directing abolitionists to purchase and distribute reprints of David Walker's *Appeal* and Henry Garnet's *Address*.

By 1850, conciliators in Congress were seeking to convince Southerners, by developing a pacifying formula, that Southern "domestic institutions," particularly slavery, were not endangered. Their efforts provoked a heated discussion in and out of Washington which in turn made for increased hostility toward the black man, who was thought to be the source of the nation's discord. Thus the increased black militancy of 1850 and after was, at one level at least, a direct response to white hostility. And the 1850 Fugitive Slave Law, part of the pacifying formula that Senators and Congressmen created, intensified the anger of blacks generally and enraged the black abolitionist leadership.

Conventions of fugitive slaves at Cazenovia, New York, and Chicago urged armed escape and killing in self-defense. Cleveland blacks declared that slaves owed no service or obedience to their masters and vowed to "protect them from recapture, whether the kidnapper comes to us as an officer of the government, or otherwise." Blacks now believed that they must "protect our right to freedom at whatever cost"; "If we have no protection we owe no allegiance." Within a month after passage of the Fugitive Slave Law, even James McCune Smith and Frederick Douglass became advocates of violence to protect fugitives. Smith looked forward to a new abolition society designed "to abolish slavery by means of the Constitution, or OTHERWISE. . . . Should there be any quarrel in the future as to the meaning of [the last two words] . . . I mean *fight*."

The Supreme Court's Dred Scott decision in 1857, declaring that blacks were not U. S. citizens, making slavery legal in every territory of the United States, and undermining if not destroying the idea of popular sovereignty, pushed Charles L. Remond further from his original position of nonviolence. Reflecting the increased mood of black militancy, Remond now proposed the preparation of an address to the slaves inviting them to rebel. The lawyer John Langston and abolitionist lecturer William Day, previously advocates of moderation, now favored resort to arms in defiance of the Fugitive Slave Law and the Dred Scott decision.

In this post-1850 context, the attraction of Canada, Haiti, and Liberia increased. Emigration, once regarded as anathema and as escapist accommodation, was viewed now as a viable alternative, for many black leaders had come to believe that their people, in order to live free, dignified lives, had but two choices —flight or violent revolution at home. It is tragic as well as ironic that white racism forced blacks who originally wished only to become an integral part of the American community into seriously considering the need for physical withdrawal. It is equally ironic that white intransigence forced upon blacks a higher tolerance for violence. For when the violence came in the form of the Civil War, it was not initiated in behalf of blacks.

The war, Lincoln said, "will be carried on so long as I am President for the sole purpose of restoring the Union." And while Lincoln eventually came to see abolition as more than a military necessity, the Emancipation Proclamation of 1863 was simply a function of logistics. Lincoln was "driven to the alternative of either surrendering the Union, and with it, the Constitution," or confiscating the slaves. After all, he wrote, "slaves are property. . . . Has there ever been any question that, by the law of war, property, both of enemies and friends, may be taken when needed?"

And the violence, though probably necessary to destroy slavery and to gain constitutional recognition of black citizenship, did little else to fulfill the abolitionists' dream of a society based on brotherly love and racial justice. In 1889, with the memory of the years of battle still fresh, and well after more than a decade of Reconstruction, Frederick Douglass could still say, as we can today:

The real question is whether American justice, American liberty, American civilization, American law and American Christianity can be made to include and protect alike and forever all American citizens. . . . It is whether this great nation shall conquer its prejudices, rise to the dignity of its professions and proceed in the sublime course of truth and liberty.

7. America Responds to Abolitionism

America's ultimate response to the abolitionists' message of justice, love, and peace was war. The abolitionists were not superhuman; they were not numerically or politically potent, and they could not prevent the society they criticized from trying to solve its problems with blood and iron. That war came did indeed have something to do with the abolitionists' activities, for they were primarily responsible for keeping the question of slavery in the forefront of American consciousness, and most historians agree with Lincoln's remark that slavery was "somehow the cause of war." But the sectional polarization that eventuated in war, although hardly conceivable without the abolitionists' activities, was the result of a complex social and political dialectic that finally had little to do with many of the important questions abolitionists raised.

Southern leaders, some of whom were sensitive to outside criticism of an institution that continued to trouble their consciences, and others who were convinced that black slavery was just and who felt their honor and self-esteem seriously threatened, overreacted to the abolitionists. In the process they played havoc with the political heritage of Southerners and Northerners alike; they violated the shared ideals and values of a libertarian society. Northern leaders, and ultimately a sizable proportion of the Northern population, responded to what they saw as the South's abuses of power by attacking the power that Southerners held. Many Southerners came to see this opposition as a serious threat to their political influence and a challenge to their honor. Their leaders responded with more political demands in an attempt to protect their self-esteem and moral legitimacy. And some Southerners, apparently a relatively small elite group of slaveholders and intellectuals, who had convinced themselves that slavery was indeed a good institution, increasingly developed a sense of Southern nationalism. This was in large part an ardent desire to protect self-esteem by bringing about (through the exacerbation of sectional tensions) secession from a political community in which the existence of black slavery was legally forbidden in some areas. In any case, increasing political demands by Southerners intensified Northerners' anti-Southernism. The cycle continued, leading to the explosion of 1860–61.

Abolitionists did convert some people in the North to full moral commitment—but not many. As Horace Greeley, editor of the New York *Tribune*, wrote in 1854, there was no "strong, pervading, overruling ANTI-Slavery sentiment in the Free States." Northerners instead developed an anti-Southernism in response to the slave power's threat to civil liberties, free labor, and free institutions generally. The North was in fact not abolitionized— it was little concerned about the immorality of slavery, the victimization of the slave, or the plight of the free black. When Northerners went to war, they did not do so for black equality or even to end slavery; they made war to put the slave power in its place. They saw themselves as saving the Union by suppressing a rebellion that was the ultimate arrogant attempt by the slave power to limit free institutions.

In the early days of the abolitionist crusade, the 1820's and early 1830's, the abolitionist attack on slavery was innocuous. Yet the slaveholders' response was virulent and frenzied, for they were still uneasy and defensive about their peculiar institution despite their highly developed racist rationale and their insistence that it was a "necessary evil."

Historians William Freehling (1965) and Charles Sellers (1960) have shown that the generation that dominated Southern life in the antebellum period had matured in an era pervaded by the values of Revolutionary liberalism. Thus for five decades after the Declaration of Independence, Southerners were openly apologetic about slavery. But the huge economic investment in it and the fear of a huge free black population always came between their awareness of the evil of slavery and the act of emancipation. Thus these Southerners clung stubbornly to the institution while continuing to feel acute guilt or at least significant tension.

Large numbers of Southerners were aware, as one antebellum writer put it, of the "detestable paradox" of their "everyday sentiments of liberty" so long as human beings were held in slavery, and many of them made the paradox painfully explicit in the Revolutionary era. The Virginia Revolutionary Convention, for example, had resolved in 1774 that the abolition of slavery was "the greatest object of desire." And the Georgia County Committee had resolved in 1775 "to show the world that we are . . . influenced by . . . a general philanthropy for all mankind" by endeavoring to eliminate "the unnatural practice of slavery."

In the post-Revolutionary era, as we have seen, most Southerners allowed the economic and social advantages of slavery to override their libertarian sentiments. And there were always some who never accepted the libertarianism or who never applied it, even as an intellectual abstraction, to blacks. Yet Southerners did not widely discuss or accept slavery as a "positive good" until after 1832, when many of their weary leaders, who themselves regarded slavery as "unnatural," tried to find a defense against outsiders who believed that "unnatural" institutions ought to be put on the road to extinction. In the 1830's, slavery became increasingly important to the Southern economy. Moreover, as we saw in Chapter 3, after the Nat Turner rebellion in 1831, the South sought more effective methods of social control over blacks and passed laws making it more difficult to manumit slaves. Southerners could no longer ease their consciences with the hope that slavery would eventually disappear. They had to invent a strong defense and make sure that everyone shared it. "It is not enough," proclaimed Calhoun's *United States Telegraph,* for the Southern people

. . . to believe that slavery has been entailed upon us by our forefathers. We must satisfy the consciences, we must allay the fears of our own people. We must satisfy them that slavery is of itself right —that it is not a sin against God—that it is not an evil, moral or political. . . . In this way, and this way only, can we prepare our own people to defend their institutions.

The slaveholders' discomfort was more than a reaction to the gulf between libertarian ideas and the institution of slavery. It probably was also a response to the day-to-day plantation experience, which so often reminded the slaveholder that the slave, despite all the racial rationalization, was, after all, a man as well as property. This indeterminate status was a daily personal problem for every master. One of the oldest justifications for slavery that Southerners offered—the need to convert the heathen —pointed up the slave's double status as both a thing—a possession—and salvageable, even perfectible, man. This was a threat to the "positive good" thesis, which depended on seeing the black as inferior. Thus, in the 1830's, proslavery men generally dropped the conversion argument and sought to justify slavery by insisting on the necessity of subordination and inequality in society.

In order to do this, for the old liberal misgivings about slavery would never completely die, it was necessary for Southern leaders to silence dissenters and critics who might disrupt their rationalizations, at home as well as in Washington. "Outside agitators" were stoned, beaten, and even killed. And as far as the domestic population was concerned, one could see the beginnings of the development of the "closed society," willing to sacrifice civil liberties on the altar of security. Because the old values were so strong, force, mob action, political manipulation, and repressive legislation had to supplement the proslavery propaganda. There were infringements on basic civil and personal rights, free speech, free press, free thought, and constitutional liberty. More and more, the South sacrificed its own traditions of democratic liberalism for a social system of neofeudal traditions in order to justify slavery and the South's superiority over a bourgeois democracy. Eventually the idea that the South was a traditional precapitalist society, wherein everyone had his place as well as his communal rights and obligations, became an important defense, as well as a counter-attack upon the free society of the North.

No doubt some men were moved to defend slavery by a sincere precapitalist ideology. The available evidence, however, appears to indicate that the proslavery defense, in the 1830's at least, did not generally reflect the master class's increasing self-confidence but, rather, its uneasy reaction to attacks on black slavery. Even George Fitzhugh, the most articulate spokesman for the Southern slavery system as a benevolent patriarchy, privately conceded that he saw immense evils in slavery. His public defense of the institution and his notion of a whole world saved from the evils of capitalism through re-enslavement were generally suspect among his fellow slaveholders. Fitzhugh's picture of a seigneurial society led by men with an aristocratic ethos was inconsistent, synthetic, and built on shaky foundations. It was embraced by many Southerners, not because they believed in it, but because they needed it so badly.

And the old ideas, although they could never lead to a serious abolitionist movement in the South, would not disappear; they kept gnawing away at the morale and self-confidence of some Southerners. This value conflict became intolerable under the mounting abolitionist attack and explains, at least in part, the violent lashing out by some Southerners in the 1830's at the mildest antislavery proposals by Northerners. By the 1840's, increasing racism throughout the United States and the phenomenal economic success of slavery allowed more Southerners than ever to believe, not just to say, that black slavery was a positive good. These Southerners, too, would lash out at antislavery proposals.

The value conflict on the part of some Southerners and the need to defend their honor and self-esteem on the part of others help to explain the desperate search for a weapon to ward off criticisms of slavery and even to prevent discussion of the question in national councils. Some Southerners thought that the idea of states rights would serve them well in this regard. South Carolina nullified a federal traiff act in 1832 on the ground that states rights justified her action. The resulting "nullification crisis" of 1832–33 did, as historian William Freehling has demonstrated, have economic roots. But many South Carolinians embraced the nullifiers' cause, as Freehling has also shown, primarily in order to win constitutional protection against the developing abolitionist crusade. If Southerners could establish the states rights principle and make it pervasive, the federal government would have little opportunity to discuss slavery, much less do anything about it.

The Governor of South Carolina, James Hamilton, Jr., wrote:

> [The South is] infested [with misguided] Missionaries; [and this] is nothing to what we shall see if we do not stand manfully at the Safety Valve of Nullification.... The same doctrines 'of the general welfare' which enable the general government to tax our industry for the benefit of industries of other sections of this Union ... would authorize the federal government to erect the *peaceful* standard of servile revolt, by establishing colonization offices in our State, to give the bounties for emancipation here, and transportation to Liberia afterwards.

Another outspoken South Carolinian said that antislavery posed a greater threat to South Carolina than tariff legislation. "Tariffs and improvement schemes are dangerous chiefly because acquiescence in those measures, on the part of the State sovereignties, sanctions . . . the constitutional right to legislate on local concerns of the States"—local concerns such as slavery.

Nullification of the tariff, then, was more than an economic battle; it was also an indirect attempt to stop the abolitionists without discussing slavery. Because of inner conflict and the need to protect honor, as well as fear that agitated discussion could lead to slave revolt, many Southerners were desperately anxious to keep the distressing subject of slavery buried. Emphasizing states rights was one way to do this. And so in the South in the 1830's there was a new stress on the rights and autonomy of communities, and less emphasis on the natural rights of all men. When states rights proved ineffective in silencing antislavery critics outside the South, Southerners simply demanded that discussion be stifled through repressive legislation at the national level.

It is important in measuring the depth and meaning of later

antislavery sentiment to note that Northern and Southern responses to the abolitionists were initially quite similar. Many Northerners simply attempted to ignore or to silence the radical critics. Connecticut, for example, passed a gag law in 1836 barring abolitionist lecturers from Congregational pulpits. And in the summer of 1835 almost every major city and town in the nation held rallies in which prominent citizens denounced abolitionists as advocates of miscegenation, dupes, fanatics, or foreign agents.

Abolitionists, after all, were attacking not only the slaveholder but also the complacent Northerner who was in effect the slaveholder's ally. Some Northerners resorted to mob violence to prevent abolitionists from making their case. There were hundreds of incidents of group action against the abolitionists in the 1830's and 1840's, most of them occurring between 1834 and 1836, when the organizational activity of the abolitionist crusade was at its zenith. According to historian Leonard Richards (1970), most incidents of mob anti-abolitionist violence were preceded by explicit planning and involved prominent community leaders.

There were also a few cases of "spontaneous" violence by mobs of mostly lower-class people. In New York City, for example, in the summer of 1834, a lower-class mob responded to a series of important abolitionist meetings by destroying abolitionist property and running riot through the black sections. Ordinary white citizens beat up blacks and burned their churches. The motivation here was apparently a fear of miscegenation or at least job competition and status diminution. While "gentlemen of property and standing" did not necessarily participate in this particular action, they did not condemn it and may even have encouraged it.

A more typical instance of mob violence occurred in Utica in 1835. Here, "action" against the abolitionists was planned for weeks, and the political and social elite of the community led and participated in the events. Lawyers, politicians, merchants, and bankers, led by Congressman Samuel Beardsley, broke up the abolitionist meeting in Utica and beat up several of the abolitionists.

Most of those who participated in the riots in the North had no direct financial stake in the survival of the slave system. But they did have a social and psychological stake in preservation of the status quo. The traditional local elites who typically made up the Northern anti-abolitionist mobs were, in the words of abolitionist Elizur Wright, Jr., men who paid homage to "wealth, power and place." The abolitionist movement was a radical force that threatened these things, because it threatened the well-ordered community. Abolitionists were seen as enemies, not only of slavery, but of the Constitution, the church, and the Union—because all of these accepted some compromise on slavery's existence. Abolitionists were proponents of dangerous ideas about equality and property rights. They sought to educate large segments of society through centrally directed organizations. They distributed free newspapers, and even children's primers. These were techniques that threatened to encroach upon the influence of traditional leadership groups.

The abolitionist movement was a threat because in its appeals it bypassed local elites and went directly to *all* men—and women! and children! and blacks! The attempt to break down distinctions among men, distinctions that gave meaning and design to the lives of the elite (despite the egalitarian rhetoric of Jacksonian America), had to be resisted. Any attack on social problems would have challenged the complacency of members of the ruling classes and created at least unconscious doubts about the moral legitimacy of their positions. But the abolitionists' radical attempt to break up the traditional patterns of power and influence throughout the land elicited even more virulent response.

Like modern militants, abolitionists were often attacked as dupes of a foreign power—in this case, England. For the local elites who ran the system could not readily admit the existence of contradictions in such basic institutions as the Constitution, the Union, and the church, all of which abolitionists so often criticized. Some alien element, like the British abolitionist movement, it was thought, must be the cause of the trouble. And as in the South, leaders in the North backed their anti-abolitionist propaganda with force. Meetings were broken up, individual abolitionists were stoned or pelted with eggs, and their property was destroyed.

After 1837 mob action against abolitionists decreased sharply. A financial depression in that year reduced the abolitionists' ability to organize and infiltrate communities, and thus they constituted less of a threat than formerly. Furthermore, mob violence was a difficult thing to sustain. A kind of exhaustion set in among anti-abolitionists, especially in places where the abolitionists had firmly established themselves. Moreover, the mob action created a great deal of anguish, even in the minds of anti-abolitionists. For while they believed in the well-ordered community, they also believed in, and boasted of, a political heritage that included freedom of speech. Concern for civil liberties gnawed at the consciences of many of those members of the local elite who participated in the violence, and moved others among the elite, and in the community generally, to condemn mob action. In fact, mob action often created a great deal of sympathy for the abolitionists, especially since abolitionists did not generally retaliate.

As the events of the 1960's in Southern cities and on college campuses all over the country have shown, violence against demonstrators for a cause often radicalizes bystanders who were previously uncommitted. So in some cases, mob action by anti-abolitionists not only created sympathy for the victims but actually made abolitionists out of the witnesses to the violence. According to psychologist Silvan Tomkins (1965) this process of "resonance" operates by arousing

> . . . vicarious distress, shame, fear, or sympathy for a victim and anger or contempt for an aggressor. As a by-product, the ideas of the victim will tend to become more influential than before such an attack.

When Dr. Henry Ingersoll Bowditch, renowned for his work in public hygiene, saw Garrison mobbed in Boston in 1835, he offered a city official help in suppressing the rioters. Bowditch was shocked when, instead of sustaining the idea of free speech,

> . . . the official [intimated that the authorities], while not wishing for a mob, rather sympathized with its object, which was to forcibly sup-

press the abolitionists. I was completely disgusted and I vowed in my heart . . . "I am an abolitionist from this very moment."

And for the next three decades, Bowditch devoted much of his energy to the cause.

Wendell Phillips possessed one of the keenest minds among the abolitionists and had everything else a Boston boy could want—wealth, good looks, family, and a Harvard education. Phillips, like Bowditch, was radicalized by the mobbing of Garrison. One afternoon not long after Phillips began his law practice, a mob rushed down Court Street in Boston dragging Garrison by a rope. As historian Richard Hofstadter relates:

> When the lawyer ran to the street and inquired why the Boston regiment was not called out to protect the victim, a bystander pointed out that most of the regiment was in the crowd. Phillips, born within sight of Bunker Hill and nurtured on the traditions of the Revolution, was an intense Boston patriot, and this violation of civil liberty in the old town revolted him. He soon drew close to the abolition movement. . . .

Phillips went on to become one of the most influential agitators and effective speakers among the abolitionists as well as a crusader for women's rights, the abolition of capital punishment, and the rights of labor. Always a thorn in the side of complacency, Phillips became an outcast to the Boston aristocracy, and eventually he had need to escape mob attack himself.

Similarly, Edmund Quincy, a man of inherited wealth and great prestige, was so stirred by the murder of Elijah Lovejoy in 1837 that he shocked the aristocratic, lettered class to which he belonged by becoming a Garrisonian abolitionist. He made his greatest contribution to the crusade as an editor and contributor, for over thirty years, to several abolitionist newspapers.

In 1833 there was only a handful of auxiliaries to the American Anti-Slavery Society; by 1835 there were 500. And by 1838, after three years of intense anti-abolitionist activity, there were 1350 auxiliaries with approximately 200,000 members.

Most witnesses to violence did not become abolitionists, but many of them did develop antislavery sympathies. After the mob attack on abolitionists in Utica, for example, over twelve hundred citizens signed a petition to abolish slavery in Washington, D.C.

If it was necessary to defend the peculiar institution with violence and the repression of civil liberties, slavery could be seen as a threat to the quality of American life. Aware of this potential, the abolitionists publicized their victimization. Alvan Stewart wrote, "The attempt of the mob at Utica to suppress free discussion . . . has been the direct means of adding thousands to the abolitionists." Whether Stewart was exaggerating or not, antislavery sentiment did increase. Between 1836 and 1838, the worst years of anti-abolitionist violence and other repressive activity, 412,000 people signed petitions to end the interstate slave trade and to abolish slavery in Washington, D.C.

The people who signed antislavery petitions but did not adopt the abolitionists' moral position nor their view of the black man as an equal might be described as fellow travelers. They developed an antipathy to slavery and were willing to work for its gradual extinction because it had a negative social, economic, and political effect on white American citizens and it contradicted middle-class concepts of freedom. This group of fellow travelers in the North began to increase when Southern leaders began to interfere with civil liberties at the national level.

In 1835 the abolitionists mounted a postal campaign to advertise their principles and goals. By the end of July, 175,000 pieces of abolitionist literature had passed through the New York post office alone. These included newspapers, pamphlets, and tracts, some especially designed for children.

Southern leaders made numerous attempts to stop the postal campaign. They boycotted abolitionist merchants like Arthur and Lewis Tappan and William Green, Jr., of New York City, who generally sold quantities of luxury goods to Southerners. They held mass anti-abolitionist rallies and condoned the mobbing of antislavery crusaders. Finally Andrew Jackson, President of the United States and titular head of the proslavery Democratic party, went before Congress in 1835 and said:

I must . . . invite your attention to the painful excitement produced in the South by attempts to circulate through the mails inflammatory appeals addressed to the passions of the slaves. . . . [M]isguided persons . . . have engaged in these unconstitutional and wicked attempts. . . . I . . . suggest . . . passing . . . a law as will prohibit, under severe penalties, the circulation in the Southern states, through the mail, of incendiary publications intended to instigate the slaves to insurrection.

John C. Calhoun, Senator from South Carolina, joined Jackson in calling for legal suppression of antislavery mail and intro-duced a bill to that effect. The idea failed to gain significant support, but Southern postmasters, apparently believing that they had the sanction of the President of the United States, removed abolitionist literature from the mails.

It is possible, too, that the irresponsible anti-abolitionist state-ments emanating from the White House at this time helped to legitimize in some people's minds violent mob action to suppress the abolitionist crusade. It was in this context that abolitionists won a great deal of attention and sympathy, for they pointed out that government censorship and proslavery violence endangered the liberties of all free men.

The mail-censorship episode created few real abolitionists— i.e., men and women concerned with the victimization of black people. But it was another factor in building support at least for limitation of the slave power. The Philadelphia *Evening Star* believed that the proposed mail laws constituted the first step in an attack upon civil liberty and characterized Calhoun's bill as "a conspiracy against the rights of freemen." The Dayton, Ohio, *Republican* wrote:

The next step will be to stop the circulation of all . . . papers . . . opposed to the administration. This done, and their censorship fairly established, we will become the *white* slaves of the masters of the black slaves of the South. Lynch law will become the exclusive law of the land, and will be enforced against any who dare to utter sentiments not in accordance with those of their masters.

In addition to the postal campaign in 1835, abolitionists ran a petition campaign. In response to this tactic some Southern Congressmen proposed a rule to "gag" discussion of slavery in the House. The evidence indicates that their motives were many and mixed, but it is apparent that some of the Southern Congressmen simply wished to avoid any discussion of the distressing subject. They did not want to be reminded of their guilt, nor did they want to accept the role of tainted, second-class participants in the political community.

At this juncture, in 1836, Southerners were powerful enough to get a bill out of committee prohibiting Congressional interference with slavery in the states and in the District of Columbia, and a gag rule providing for automatic rejection of slavery petitions. But rejection would not foreclose discussion. Militant Southern Congressmen denounced the proposed bill (some historians think that they were already aiming at secession, purposely manipulating the situation in order to elicit a Northern reaction that would help them unify the South) and agitated for a stronger gag rule—one that would automatically table the petitions without discussion. The original gag rule was passed in 1836, but it had to be renewed every two years. And by 1840, Southerners were able to prohibit the House of Representatives from even receiving antislavery petitions, which effectively cut off discussion of slavery in Congress. Of course, Southerners could not do this alone, and at first many Northerners, mostly Democrats, cooperated for the sake of party unity. But every time the gag rule came up for renewal, Northern support decreased. By 1844, an overwhelming Northern majority defeated the gag rule for the first time.

Here was an indication that Northern politicians were willing to take a sectional, or anti-slave-power, position on some questions at least. Only after the first gag rule was passed did the petition campaign really mushroom. People who would not have signed an antislavery petition in 1835 rushed to sign when their constitutional right to do so appeared to be threatened.

As in the postal controversy, the abolitionists attempted to link their crusade with the cause of free speech. The wealthy Boston merchant and Garrisonian abolitionist Francis Jackson said in 1835:

Mobs and gag laws ... betray the essential rottenness of the cause

... they are meant to strengthen. ... Happily, one point seems already to be gaining universal assent, that slavery cannot long survive free discussion. Hence the efforts of the friends and apologists of slavery to break down this right. And hence the immense stake, which the enemies of slavery hold, in behalf of freedom and mankind, in its preservation. The contest is therefore substantially between liberty and slavery.

Congressman John Quincy Adams, former President of the United States, vigorously led the fight against the gag rule in the House. He was not an abolitionist but he did hold "the resolution to be in direct violation of the Constitution of the United States, of the rules of this House, and of the rights of my constituents." The more aggressive the Southerners grew in defense of slavery, the more Adams saw the need for limitation of the slave power—a power that was becoming, according to the former President, "the disgrace and degradation of my country, trampling in the dust the first principle of human liberty."

And Joshua Giddings agreed in 1842: "The Slave interest has assiduously crept into our whole policy . . . invaded the sanctity of the Post Office, degraded our Patriotism, . . . frightened our Statesmen and controlled the nation." Despite party loyalty, the fear of disunion, and strong economic interests, an anti-slave-power and even an anti-Southern sentiment was obviously developing among Northern political leaders.

The results of the Mexican War (1846–48) encouraged the growth of this sentiment. Although Calhoun and other pro-slavery Democrats had warned the Senate against conquering Mexico, abolitionists and some of their fellow travelers saw Texas annexation (1845) and the Mexican War as part of the "slave-power conspiracy" to extend slave territory. Still, for most men, party loyalty appeared to be more binding than sectional affiliation. In the Senate, for example, after the election of expansionist James K. Polk, Whigs from both North and South voted against Texas annexation, 23–3, and Democrats North and South voted for it, 24–2.

But the prospect of gaining 500,000 square miles of territory as a result of the war raised the old question of the federal government's role in respect to slavery. And party loyalty, on this question at least, eroded in 1846, when Congressman David Wilmot, a Democrat from Pennsylvania, introduced an anti-slavery rider to an administration bill providing two million dollars to facilitate negotiations with Mexico. Slavery, according to the final version of the Wilmot Proviso, was to be prohibited from all newly acquired territory. The House defeated the proviso. But in this vote, unlike the Texas vote, *all* Northern Whigs voted for slavery restriction, all Southern Whigs against it; most Northern Democrats voted for slavery restriction, and all Southern Democrats voted against.

The perfect sectional division among the Whigs reflected the sensitivity of Northern Whigs to the slavery question, which was greater than that of Northern Democrats. One explanation is that most Liberty party voters were former Whigs, and the Whigs wanted to attract them back to the party. (William Goodell estimated that 80 per cent of the voting abolitionists had previously been affiliated with the Whigs. No contemporary estimate was less than 65 per cent, and modern research has generally borne this out.)

In some measure, the original Liberty party strategy was working. The Whigs in the North, and even some Democrats there, were being pushed to take antislavery positions more openly. Democrats in the South, however, harassed Southern Whigs to identify with their section rather than with their "Northern-oriented party." By 1846 it appears that this tactic on the part of Southern Democrats was also working, if only on the slavery question.

The issue had tremendous public appeal, North and South. The territories in question were of dubious practical importance. They were not particularly suited to slave labor, and slaveholders showed great reluctance to emigrate there with their slaves. Even John C. Calhoun agreed with President Polk that slavery would probably never exist in the territories to be acquired and claimed that he had no desire to see it extended there. But Calhoun came out strongly against the Wilmot Proviso, which in his view threatened Southern rights—and with them the self-confidence and moral validity of the Southern "way of life."

By now, many Northerners saw the "slave power" as a political ruling class whose arrogance needed deflating. And Northern antislavery Congressmen in both parties were at least partially motivated by the desire to "stand up to the South." Wilmot himself said to Southern Congressmen during debate, "We will conquer you, drive you to the wall, nail you there!"

The antislavery Congressman Joshua Giddings, commenting on the sectional nature of Northern voting on the Wilmot Proviso, said, "I now see the mighty deep of public indignation called forth against . . . the encroachments of the slave power. I now for the first time . . . see the slave power falter . . . before the combined denunciation of Northern democrats and Northern whigs."

Northerners were interested in liberating their section from the control of the slave power. Many Northerners in addition to the abolitionists had come to see the injustice of slavery. But they were not willing to risk the disruption of their parties and disunion or to take on what they regarded as other terrifying consequences of abolition, such as the problem of the freed black. The nonextension formula of the Wilmot Proviso was a perfect device for balancing multiple needs. Advocates of the proviso were expressing, through their stand, a sincere but safe antislavery sentiment, as well as a growing anti-Southernism. At the same time, most Northerners peremptorily dismissed the idea that their ultimate aim was abolition.

But it was not fear of abolition primarily that motivated the intense and spontaneous Southern reaction to the possibility of slavery restriction. One of the most troubling aspects of the proviso for Southerners, including those who suffered no value conflict, convinced they were "good men living in a good society," was its implicit assumption that Southern society, with its slaveholding system, was morally inferior to that of the North. Peter V. Daniel of Virginia, Associate Justice of the U. S. Supreme Court, wrote that the proviso contained greater dangers

... than any that can flow from mere calculation of political influence, or of profit arising from a distribution of territory. It is the view of the case which pretends to an insulting exclusiveness or superiority on the one hand, and denounces a degrading inequality or inferiority on the other, which says in effect to the Southern man, Avaunt! you are not my equal, and hence are to be excluded as carrying a moral taint with you. Here is at once the extinction of all fraternity, of all sympathy, of all endurance even; the creation of animosity fierce, implacable, undying. It is the unmitigated outrage which I venture to say, there is no true Southron from the schoolboy to the octogenarian, who is not prepared for any extremity in order to repel it.

After the Wilmot Proviso debates, Southern Democrats claimed that they were the only party that represented the interests of the South. Some Northerners went so far as to claim that no self-respecting human being could live in a society dominated by the institution of slavery. And Southerners increasingly defended slavery as a positive good. Slaveholders, whether or not they favored slavery expansion, denounced any abridgement of the *right* to take slaves to the territories. In fact, Southerners became so defensive on this point that they reversed a constitutional position they had taken in 1820 on the Missouri question, and now denied the power of Congress to restrict slavery in the territories.

In short, the momentous question of the federal government's role in respect to slavery was reopened, and sectional tensions increased. Most important, large numbers of people were involved, and thus the tensions now had the potential for becoming explosive.

In fact, the votes for the Free Soil party in 1848, and later for the Republican party, indicated that many Northerners would support an antislavery party—as long as it did not demand immediate and total abolition of slavery or political and social equality for freed blacks. According to a leading student of Northern antislavery political parties, Eric Foner (1965),

The party's platform was so broad that it could gain the support of those who opposed slavery in order to prevent Negroes from fleeing North and those who desired to keep the territories free from the presence of the Negro slave, as well as the veteran anti-slavery men with their moral abhorrence of the institution, and Northerners worried by the great influence of the "Slave Power" in the federal government. The Free Soil party numbered in its ranks the most vulgar racists and the most determined supporters of Negro rights, as well as shades of opinion between these extremes. It was the only anti-slavery position that could accomplish this because the question of Negro rights, potentially such a divisive issue, was simply avoided in its national platform.

While the Free Soil party was forming, the major parties were trying to put their Northern and Southern wings back together. Thus, the Whigs, who had been accused of treason to the South, nominated Zachary Taylor, a Southern slaveholder, for the Presidency. And the Democrats, charged with knuckling under to the South and fearful of losing key Northern electoral blocs, nominated Michigan Senator Lewis Cass. Perhaps because of these attempts by the rival parties to ameliorate the sectional rift, the Free Soil party failed to carry a single state. Nevertheless, North and South remained relatively self-conscious.

The Free Soil campaign, run by former Democratic President Martin Van Buren on a platform of opposition to slavery expansion and domination of the slave power, could not help but strain the bond between Northern and Southern Democrats. One of Senator John P. Hale's constituents spoke for many Northerners when he congratulated Hale for affiliating with the Free Soilers: "I feel *proud*, sir, that we have a Senator . . . who is not afraid or ashamed, to stand up for the rights of the North." And Van Buren himself observed to a colleague that the events of 1848 "have produced impressions which neither you nor I will live to see eradicated."

But sectional self-consciousness might have remained passive for a long time had not gold been discovered in California in 1849. By 1850 enough people had followed the lure to that Pacific territory to apply for admission to the Union as a state— a free state. The debate over California's admission was probably the most acrimonious in American Congressional history to that point. Southerners constantly made reference to the insulting Wilmot Proviso and how California's admission as a free state would fulfill the proviso's intent. This was curious, however, because the proviso had to do only with territories before they became states, and the states-rights South did not propose to force California into the Union as a slave state despite the wishes of her population. But the South did do something almost as arrogant as far as the North was concerned. The South held up the admission of California pending some concession on the question of slavery in the territories.

Finally, a bill was passed admitting California as a free state and organizing the other territories of the Mexican cession without reference to slavery. This was a tacit approval of popular sovereignty. The concept of popular sovereignty fixed no moral stigma on slavery, the slaveholder, or the South. Thus Southerners could accept it with dignity, if not with satisfaction.

The South, in addition, was able to extract from the Congress a new, stronger Fugitive Slave Law, prejudicial to the alleged as well as the real fugitive. It prohibited him from testifying in his own behalf, and it paid the federal marshall judging a case more for finding in favor of the slave hunter than for ruling in favor of the fugitive. The law also gave the marshall power to impress people into slave hunting.

Both Southern apologists and antislavery men admitted that their respective positions on the law were based mostly on sectional pride. The law satisfied the South to some extent that it was still influential, while the North was incensed at this new homage to the slave power as well as at the threat to civil liberties.

Ordinary Northern citizens sometimes resisted enforcement of the law. Many of these citizens *were* concerned to some extent with the plight of the fugitive. For some resistance may even have been a psychologically significant stride toward commitment to abolitionism. But for most it meant simply defiance of the slave power, which by now appeared to be the enemy of the Republic.

Attempts to enforce the Fugitive Slave Law in the North between 1850 and 1854 kept antislavery sentiment alive if not thriving in an otherwise placid period. The debates over California had been so heated that many political leaders from both sections had drawn back for fear of destroying the Union, and a relative calm settled over the political scene. This calm was shattered in 1853-54, when Senator Stephen A. Douglas of Illinois, wishing to develop a central route for the transcontinental railroad, introduced bills to organize the Nebraska territory.

Nebraska lay north of the 36°30′ parallel, the compromise line drawn as a result of the 1820 debate over the admission of Missouri. Territory north of this line was to be free. Thus most Southerners voted against the bill to organize Nebraska, and it was defeated. In order for Douglas to attract Southern votes, he accepted, on the advice of several Southern Senators, an amendment to his bill which would repeal the Missouri compromise!

Douglas' bill passed in this form, striking from the statute books a compromise of over thirty years' standing. Many Northerners had grown up believing that this compromise was in some way part of the Constitution, or at least immune from mere legislative change. Thus, as far as they were concerned, the repeal was another example of arrogant Southern abuse of power.

A constituent wrote to Massachusetts Senator Charles Sumner that the enforcement of the Fugitive Slave Law in the Anthony Burns case in 1854 (see pp. 94, 108), in combination with "the passage of the nefarious Nebraska bill, had done more than anything else to unite the good men of all parties [in the North] in a common sentiment of hostility to the encroachments of the slave power."

President Franklin Pierce signed the Nebraska bill, and President James Buchanan after him grossly misapplied the power of his office to make sure that the states to be carved out of that territory would be sympathetic to the slave interests. In 1857, he encouraged Congress to admit Kansas with a proslavery state constitution that was obviously a result of force and fraud. Buchanan was interested in holding the Democratic party together and feared a Southern bolt. However, he underestimated the reaction of Northerners, who saw that Congress and now the Presidency were under the control of the "slave interest."

William Goodell had written in 1855 that the "slave interest" not only wanted to maintain slavery but wished to foist it on the nation, destroy civil liberties, and set up a nationwide aristocracy. It began to appear to many Northerners, including large numbers of Democrats who eventually joined the Republican party, that the abolitionist idea of a slave-power conspiracy was not imaginary.

The conspiracy theory was helped along in 1857 by the Supreme Court's ruling in the Dred Scott case. Scott was a slave who had been taken to the free territory of Minnesota, as well as to the free state of Illinois. Scott, although he was in slave-state Missouri at the time, with the help of others brought suit for his freedom on the basis of his previous stays in nonslave territory. The Court ruled that blacks were not citizens and therefore could not sue in federal courts. The justices could have stopped at that, but they thought they could solve the slavery question once and for all. They further ruled that since Dred Scott was again a resident of Missouri, his Illinois trip had no lasting effect on his status. Most important, however, was the final ruling. The majority of the justices decided that Minnesota was not free territory, because the Missouri Compromise, which had declared it free, was unconstitutional. According to the Fifth Amendment to the Constitution, the federal government cannot deprive citizens of property without due process of law. The justices interpreted this to mean that neither the Congress nor its territorial creations could rule against slavery. Slavery was henceforth legal in all the territories of the United States regardless of the wishes of their respective populations.

Many Northerners assumed that the Court had been captured by the slave-power conspiracy, since a majority of justices were indeed from the South. In fact, however, there was not enough unity in the South to pull off such a conspiracy, but the slaveholders did constitute a powerful interest.

As early as 1854, informal quasi-political groups, calling themselves "Friends of Freedom," had been forming in the North to confront that slaveholder interest. In 1856 they held a national convention and took the name Republican. The new political organization was made up of former Whigs, dissident Democrats, and some Liberty men. By 1860 it was to be the majority party in the North, winning approximately 54 per cent of the electorate's vote. But it is important to note that in 1860 the

North was not a monolith of antislavery sentiment: 46 per cent of the electorate still voted against the Republican party. The coexisting values of unionism and antislavery divided the Northern mind and confused its allegiance.

Moreover, the Republican party represented more than antislavery. Growth of the party was fostered to an important extent by a surge of feeling against Catholicism. Between 1847 and 1855, the annual rate of immigration to America had risen sharply, bringing many Irish and German Catholics to our shores. In an America already suffering from sectional tensions and a lack of confidence in the survival power of its republican experiment, this large influx of numbers of people with radical cultural differences increased insecurity. Anti-Catholicism, or nativism, proved to be a powerful force at the polls. Many politicians thought they saw the wave of the future and took bold, open anti-Catholic stands. Nativist political parties began to form even prior to the local Friends of Freedom (later Republican parties), and by 1854–55, they had achieved a great deal of power. They captured, for example, the state legislatures of New York and Massachusetts during this period.

In many states the Republican party and the Nativist party (sometimes known as the Native American or Know-Nothing party) merged, keeping the label Republican. For the slave power and the international power of the Catholic church were similar enemies in that, to the middle-class democracy of the North, both represented vestiges of un-American authoritarianism. By 1860 the Republican party emerged as an anti-Catholic as well as anti-Southern political force.

The Republican party program, moreover, had only one antislavery plank—exclusion of slavery from the territories—and this was to be a distant goal since the Supreme Court had only recently proclaimed slavery legal in all territories. Furthermore, the party propaganda gives the impression that 1856 marked the zenith of the Republicans' antislavery crusade; from then until about 1862 antislavery was subordinated to a number of planks which, in good American tradition and style, promised something for everyone.

But whatever its shortcomings, the Republican party was the

only major political force reflecting the antislavery sentiment of the North. And since recent political history taught the Republicans that an antislavery party could be successful only if it did not touch on demands for political and social equality for free blacks, the party worked hard to dissociate itself from these abolitionist doctrines.

In the East, Republicans tried to ignore the racial problem as much as possible. But because of strong Northern anti-black feeling, Republicans were often put on the defensive. The party's stand in such situations was to emphasize the needs of free white labor. Sometimes Republicans resorted to an implicit racism. Horace Greeley wrote in the *Tribune* "that all the unoccupied territory of the United States, and such as they may hereafter acquire, . . . [should] be reserved for the benefit and occupation of the white Caucasian race—a thing which cannot be except by the exclusion of slavery."

In the West, dislike for the black was more intense than in the East. And astute Republican leaders often used that dislike for their advantage. Sometimes enmity toward the black race was the *only* reason given for opposing slavery. Oregon Republicans, in an 1857 broadside on the slavery question, resolved to limit their efforts "to the sole and single object of making Oregon a free state as the best and only means of securing it to the white race." Westerners considered even the very limited slavery that could take root there most undesirable. For where slavery was weakest, there was the greatest possibility of emancipation, which would present whites with the free-black problem and all its social and psychological implications. Politicians in the West knew that almost 80 per cent of the people of Illinois, Indiana, Oregon, and Kansas (states with antislavery constitutions) had voted to exclude the free black from their borders. And some Republicans were willing to campaign on racist programs of this kind to attract voters.

Still, Republican racism was mainly defensive, unlike the racism of Northern Democrats, who exhibited a crude, unbridled Negrophobia. Thus some abolitionists saw the popular support for the Republican party as a step in the right direction. In fact, many gave the party both votes and money. Elizur

Wright, Jr., believed that "the average sentiment of the party is more anti-slavery than the platform, and the sentiment of the most active and efficient leaders still more so." Gerrit Smith actually contributed $500 to the party in 1856. Yet he continued to criticize the Republican party and to support a Radical Abolition party, whose platform called for abolition of slavery in the states as well as in the territories, and for civil rights for blacks. Garrison's *Liberator* said that the success of the Republican party "will do no slight service to the cause of freedom; and to that extent, and for that reason, it has our sympathies and best wishes."

William Seward, a moderate antislavery man regarded with favor by some abolitionists, was the frontrunner for the Republican presidential nomination early in 1860. When he was overtaken at the Republican National Convention in the summer of 1860 by the relatively unknown Abraham Lincoln, a crisis was created for those abolitionists who were supporting the Republicans. They discovered that Lincoln had said in 1854:

My first impulse would be to free all the slaves, and send them to Liberia,—to their own native land. But . . . [this] is impossible. . . . What then? Free them, and make them politically and socially our equals? My own feelings will not admit of this.

Yet, at various times, he had branded the institution of slavery as a "moral, social and political wrong . . . an unqualified evil to the negro, to the white man, to the Soil, and to the State."

Lincoln, like his party, was plainly not an abolitionist, but he was just as plainly against slavery. Some abolitionists recognized that this was the best they could hope for in the circumstances. Southerners recognized that this was the worst they could expect. And when Lincoln was elected, several Southern states felt impelled to secede.

There were attempts to reassure the South that emancipation was not an aim of Lincoln or his party. Greeley wrote, "Never on earth did the Republican Party propose to abolish slavery." And Congress passed a constitutional amendment guaranteeing slavery in the states against interference by the federal government. Within months three Northern states had ratified the Amendment. Indeed, evidence indicates that most Southern leaders knew that there was no powerful political group in the North that *strongly* desired and would *seriously* work for abolition of slavery.

But again, as in the political battles of the 1840's and 1850's, as much as the prospect of abolition, the South objected to policies and statements by powerful, prestigious American leaders that implied the South's moral inferiority. To the South, Lincoln's antislavery statements and the Republican policy of restriction implied just this.

The South's inner conflict on slavery and the need to protect honor and self-esteem had produced belligerent dogmatism in the 1830's, 1840's, and 1850's; in 1860 it produced a readiness to follow the advocates of aggressive action who had long since been on the scene. But war was dependent on more than the South's decision to secede. The Republican administration could have decided to let the South go peacefully. There were, as we have seen, advocates of peaceful secession, including most of the abolitionists. But such a course was politically inconceivable. The national administration could not afford, in the land that represented the "last true hope of mankind," to admit that the experiment in republican government was failing; it could not afford violation of the territorial integrity of the United States; it could not afford to ignore the mystique of Union.

Furthermore, the Republican administration, in its attempt to prevent secession, was motivated by its own ideology, which emphasized, as Eric Foner has demonstrated (1970), mobility and choice, free labor, civil liberties—the values of a growing bourgeois democracy. Many Northerners believed that the maintenance of the Union, with its image, its national power, its national wealth, was necessary to fulfill these values. Thus, the South would not be allowed to go, even though this course would finally resolve the slavery dispute.

The abolitionists had succeeded in making the slaveholders appear to be the enemy of the Republic. The behavior of the

South in response to abolitionist and antislavery criticism precipitated a political crisis over slavery and made antislavery sentiment popular in the North. Yet in the 1850's, when influential major party politicians took the leadership in the antislavery crusade, the old egalitarian ideals of the abolitionists were obscured. This meant that racial inequality was not to be among those problems finally resolved by the war.

8. War and the Fruits of War

There yet remains a great work to be done to eradicate the spirit of slavery and the spirit of caste so deeply rooted in the heart.

—AMOS DRESSER, 1874

The abolitionists had initiated a cycle of events that brought the North to recognize the injustice of slavery and wish to limit the slave power. Ultimately, during the Civil War, the abolitionists helped to convince Northerners that emancipation was both a necessary war measure and consistent with the ideology of democracy they espoused against the neo-aristocracy of the South. On one level, then, the abolitionists were immensely successful. Working in a hostile environment, with extremely limited resources, they achieved one of their most important objectives—the destruction of slavery—in little more than a generation since the rise of immediatism. But in the crucible of war, many of the humanitarian concerns of the abolitionists were overshadowed by patriotism, love of glory, and the needs of the state. And so, on the "Negro question" and on the question of coercion, which were part of the larger question of the meaning of America, they changed few minds and hearts. From the 1770's to the 1870's, the abolitionists shared the dream that

America was a new start for mankind, a place uncorrupted by the sins of the European past, a place where the human race could remake itself through the power of love. But they were unable to convince most Americans, involved in a drive for power and gain, to adopt that dream and accept black men as brothers, or even as fellow citizens.

During the war and Reconstruction, the abolitionists helped to bring about some notable legislation and constitutional changes in regard to racial discrimination. And although these changes were rarely enforced at the time, according to historians C. Vann Woodward (1967), James McPherson (1964), Kenneth Stampp (1965), and others, they were a necessary foundation for today's black liberation movement.

That the abolitionists did not realize significant parts of their vision in their own time was partly their fault. Many of them never completely dissociated themselves from early paternalistic motives, and not many perceived that collective action and massive social planning were essential for implementation of their ideas. Moreover, their support of the Republican party and ultimately of the war trapped the abolitionists into defending a nationalistic policy that contradicted much of their prewar ideology. But the bulk of the blame lies with a society that refused to hear what the abolitionists were really saying.

Only as the Civil War progressed did Northern society begin to recognize even the abolition of slavery as a legitimate goal. The abolitionists had tried to teach that emancipation was not only an expedient war measure but the first step of a revolution toward an egalitarian, noncoercive society; the North chose to view emancipation at first as a military necessity and ultimately as a fulfillment of the ideology of a free bourgeois society.

The abolitionists, as we have seen, did not want war. The use of violence to accomplish their goal was to many of them immoral and also, they thought, inexpedient. "If the slaves are to be freed by war," the nonresistant clergyman Adin Ballou asked,

what is to be done with them for the next hundred years? It

would take at least a century to educate them out of the ferocity engendered by such conflict. How are they to be employed, trained for liberty, and organized into well-ordered communities? And above all how is this work to be accomplished with the great mass of the whites in the country full of horror, loathing and revenge toward them? . . . Can't we wait the operations of a more peaceful process? . . . It may seem hard to wait, but if we do not wait, we shall do worse.

But when war came despite their efforts, many abolitionists were convinced that slavery, at least, could be brought to an end in the process. They hoped, as the *Anti-Slavery Standard* wrote, that although "this outburst of spirit and enthusiasm at the north may spring chiefly from indignation at the wrongs of the white man, . . . it will nonetheless finally right those of the black man." The Pennsylvania abolitionist J. Miller McKim was confident that the conflict was "to be an abolition war. The South has elected to give it this character. . . . The North has not been and is not yet prepared for final action on this question; but she has no alternative."

But the abolitionists had their work cut out for them. After all, as the Republican New York *Tribune* had unequivocally stated, "This war is in truth a war for the preservation of the Union, not for the destruction of slavery. . . . We believe that slavery has nothing to fear from a Union triumph." The abolitionists therefore believed it necessary to exploit every opportunity during the war to push Lincoln and the Congress toward an antislavery position. Like John Jay, they feared that "If the slavery question is ignored and the people are taught to look upon it [the war] as a mere sectional struggle for power, it will sink to a mere political question in which they will take but little interest." Moreover, many abolitionists believed, with reason, that the peculiar institution would be more firmly entrenched if the war ended without destroying slavery. Some of them therefore gave up the pacifism that was at the heart of their social philosophy. And several—including Garrison and Tappan—were logically maneuvered into hoping that the war, despite its horror, would go on until slavery was completely eliminated. And while Garrisonian societies avoided directly calling for enlistments, many individual abolitionists encouraged enlistment in the armed forces, especially as the government gradually increased its commitment to antislavery.

Of course, those abolitionists who had never taken a strongly principled position against violence supported the war without much hesitation. For example, Massachusetts abolitionist Thomas Wentworth Higginson, who had urged the use of physical force to rescue fugitive Anthony Burns, became colonel of the first regiment of freed slaves in the Union forces. Nevertheless, there were those who remained skeptical. "Even should . . . [slaves] be emancipated, merely as a 'war necessity,'" wrote Lydia Maria Child, "everything *must* go wrong, if there is no heart or conscience on the subject. . . ." But the rush of events during 1861–62 made it unlikely that many abolitionists, with a chance to see the first stage of their program fulfilled, would stop to brood about future problems.

To win Northern favor for emancipation, abolitionists had to use every argument at their disposal, and so, uncomfortable as it was for some of them, they exploited the notion of "military necessity." There were thousands of slaves doing the heavy physical labor of the Southern army. They built fortifications, dug trenches, and drove teams. The abolitionists pointed out that this was a significant asset to the Confederacy. "Why? Oh! Why in the name of all that is rational," Frederick Douglass asked, "does our Government allow its enemies this powerful advantage?" Emancipation thus would deprive the South of a formidable source of strength. And the addition of black troops to the Union armies might (and eventually did) give the North a significant edge. The *Anti-Slavery Standard* put the argument succinctly: "Success in the War, without Emancipation, is a Military Impossibility. . . ."

Abolitionists also pointed out that neither England nor Europe could have much sympathy with the North's cause if it were fighting only for political dominion. Abolition as a war aim, however, would give the struggle ideological justification and gain the respect of foreign powers.

Even if they could convince the North that emancipation

was a military necessity, abolitionists knew they had to prove to legal-minded Americans that emancipation was also constitutional. To that end, they emphasized the President's constitutionally granted power to confiscate property in time of war. On the day after the North's surrender of Fort Sumter, on April 13, 1861, abolitionists began urging Lincoln and Congress, through speeches, letters, petitions, and personal confrontation, to proclaim emancipation under the war power.

The antislavery crusaders were disheartened when, on July 4, 1861, the President renewed his pledge not to interfere with slavery in the states. Their disappointment intensified three weeks later, when Congress, still seeking reconciliation, resolved almost unanimously that "this war is not waged upon our part . . . for any purpose . . . of overthrowing or interfering with the rights or established institutions of . . . Southern states."

The abolitionists' offensive against slavery began to have more effect on the people of the North when the Union forces, on July 21, 1861, suffered their first significant defeat at the battle of Bull Run in Virginia. The argument that the ability to call on slave labor gave the South a significant advantage seemed now to make more sense. And on August 30, 1861, Union General John C. Fremont issued a proclamation freeing the slaves of every rebel in the state of Missouri.

Abolitionists responded immediately with praise. Gerrit Smith pointedly informed Lincoln in a public letter that "this step of General Fremont is the first unqualified and purely right one, in regard to our colored population, which has taken place during the war." The President was unimpressed by Smith's argument; he revoked Fremont's order.

Abolitionists realized now that they had underestimated the difficulty of moving the administration toward emancipation. They launched a more intensive propaganda offensive. Sharp criticism of Lincoln began to appear more frequently in abolitionist writings. And a number of new organizations emerged which aimed at universal emancipation.

Abolitionists knew that the North was divided on the question of emancipation. They believed, however, that most Northerners, because of the ineffectiveness of the Union war effort, were convinced that emancipation was necessary to weaken the Confederacy. The abolitionists worked to add an ideological dimension to Northern emancipation sentiment. At the same time they hoped to advertise that sentiment to the political leadership. To this end, Emancipation Leagues in Boston, New York, and Washington, D.C., sent out broadsides, ran petition campaigns, and sponsored lecture series.

Abolitionist speakers were in great demand throughout the North. Wendell Phillips and Frederick Douglass spoke to thunderous applause in cities where they had a year or two earlier been mobbed. The New York *Tribune* estimated that during the winter and spring of 1861–62 no fewer than 5,000,000 people heard or read Wendell Phillips' antislavery speeches.

Although the President and several leading members of Congress attended abolitionist lectures in Washington, Lincoln and most of the Republican party remained "anxious and careful" that the war did not "degenerate into a violent and remorseless revolutionary struggle." The Northern population was increasingly open to the idea of emancipation, but it was difficult for politicians to measure whether this was a stronger force than white apprehension over the threat of a massive black invasion of the North after emancipation.

Thus, from March to July, 1862, the administration moved haltingly in the direction of emancipation. Republican congressmen recommended compensated emancipation in the border states; Army officers were prohibited from returning fugitive slaves; slavery was abolished with compensation in the District of Columbia; and slavery was prohibited in the territories.

Republicans also voted heavily against discrimination in hiring mail carriers, and heavily for the establishment of an institution for the education of colored youth in Washington, D.C. This indicated that some politicians at least expected future emancipation and recognized a need to prepare for it. At the same time, however, the administration continued to enforce the Fugitive Slave Law in the District of Columbia, and the House defeated a bill for the confiscation and emancipation of all slaves belonging to rebel masters. Five Massachusetts votes provided the margin of defeat.

Not surprisingly, Republicans followed a prudent course between abolitionist demands and Northern racism. Their bow to anti-black sentiment was in large measure defensive. They felt that in order to have the power to abolish slavery, they must be politically successful. And this meant dissociating the party from the idea of equality. Thus, as the party moved toward emancipation, Lincoln and other Republicans insisted that they were not trying to "Africanize" the North. Congressman George Julian and Senator Salmon P. Chase advanced the theory that emancipation would actually decrease the North's black population. Northern blacks, these Republican leaders predicted, would be attracted by the more congenial, "natural" environment of the post-emancipation South, and would emigrate there.

Abolitionists in the meantime pushed the idea of black liberation. In the summer of 1862, Susan B. Anthony and Angelina Grimké Weld went on whirlwind petition and speaking tours to build up support for emancipation. Throughout the North, abolitionists and Radical Republicans followed their example. And finally on September 22, 1862, in the hope of persuading some Southern states to return to the fold and depriving the rest of black manpower, President Lincoln issued a preliminary proclamation declaring that all slaves in areas still in rebellion on January 1, 1863, were "then, thenceforward, and forever free."

Military events were indeed decisive. But Lincoln was still a reluctant emancipator. "After the commencement of hostilities," he wrote to one of his generals in January, 1863, "I struggled for nearly a year and a half to get along without touching the institution." And Lincoln's friend and law partner said: "When [the President] freed the slaves there was no heart in it."

In the face of the ineffectiveness of the Union Army, Lincoln feared that Radicals in Congress who wanted abolition of slavery and even limited integration would openly attempt to embarrass the government in the conduct of the war. Bills were impending requiring the administration to draft into the armed forces not only white men but black men, including all able-bodied slaves in the border states. There is also some evidence that Lincoln believed that the Radicals would take the extreme step of withholding war supplies if their bills were vetoed. Had the abolitionists and Radicals not been effectively educating Northern opinion for over a year on the necessity of emancipation, the President might not have felt the pressure to act.

The Proclamation actually went no further than two clumsy and unenforceable confiscation acts that Congress had passed in 1861 and 1862. And some abolitionists, hoping to get a more sweeping emancipation, denounced the Proclamation as an example of "circumlocution and delay." But once the Proclamation went into effect, they hailed it as "a great historic event, ... momentous and beneficent in its far-reaching consequences."

After the initial euphoria had dissipated, abolitionists realized that the Proclamation did not apply to loyal slave states and, moreover, while legitimate in wartime, might be challenged once the war was over. Thus they campaigned for a constitutional amendment to end slavery. By July, 1864, two thousand men, women, and children had collected 400,000 signatures on petitions for an abolition amendment. This was an impressive achievement, and the antislavery Senators Charles Sumner and Henry Wilson assured the abolitionists that the petition campaign lent great assistance in the battle for Congressional approval of an abolition amendment. Republicans had only a bare majority in the House, where a two-thirds vote was necessary for passage. However, the re-election in 1864 of Lincoln, who had become, through the Emancipation Proclamation, a symbol of freedom, convinced several Democrats that the public wanted emancipation; they therefore abstained or changed their votes, enabling the House to pass the Thirteenth Amendment on January 31, 1865.

Lincoln himself worked very hard to secure a two-thirds vote, perhaps indicating the capacity for moral growth ascribed to him by some historians. The Amendment abolishing slavery everywhere in the United States went out to the states and was ratified before the end of the year.

Republicans and abolitionists had campaigned for emancipation on different grounds. The Republicans backed their antislavery petition with racist arguments while abolitionists argued for racial justice. The politicians, after all, faced an actively anti-black constituency whose support they could not afford to alienate. In 1860, Northerners continued to deny the ballot to 93 per cent of the 225,000 blacks living in the free states. Everywhere in the North whites had erected barriers to black employment and had set severe limitations to the protection of a black person's life, liberty, and property.

While the early years of the war increased antislavery sentiment, they did little to improve Northern attitudes toward the black. In fact, as we have seen, the fear of a post-emancipation black invasion often hardened Negrophobia. Many Republican politicians, unwilling to give up their sincere antislavery goals, had been forced into taking racist positions to allay the fears of white Northerners. Lincoln, for example, asked Northerners who expressed anxiety over black migration, "Can not the North decide for itself whether to receive them?" The President was implying that Northern state legislatures could imitate some of the Western states by passing black-exclusion laws.

Republicans, to allay Northern fears, also talked about black removal. One abolitionist who toured upstate New York in the spring of 1862 reported that "unfriendly expressions against the colored people were never more common. . . . Many Republicans unite with Democrats in cursing the 'niggers' and in declaring that the slaves, if possibly emancipated by the war, must be removed from the country." Congress actually appropriated $600,000 in 1862 to provide for the voluntary emigration of blacks who were freed by the District of Columbia Act and by the confiscation acts. And between 1861 and 1863 Lincoln made several other colonization proposals.

Abolitionists lashed out at the President's proposals. At the end of 1861, Boston's black leaders resolved

> . . . that when we wish to leave the United States we can find and pay for that territory which shall suit us best, . . . that when we are ready to leave, we shall be able to pay our own expenses of travel. . . . [T]hat we don't want to go now, . . . that if anybody wants us to go, they must compel us.

White abolitionists agreed with many of their black colleagues that colonization proposals were "twattle and trash," "absurd and preposterous." And they realized anew that final victory depended on convincing whites of the equality of the races. Thus the abolitionists brought their argument about the black's racial character to a new intensity between 1861 and 1865. They used every source at their disposal to demonstrate the essential unity and equality of man. They quoted from the Bible, cited secular historical examples, and asked men and women to examine the obvious facts of their own experience. Over and over, abolitionists emphasized environmentalism, explaining black "disabilities" as the brutalizing effect of enslavement. They often quoted European biologists, whose findings on racial differences enabled abolitionists to argue forcefully and accurately that science had failed to prove the black innately inferior.

Frederick Douglass summed up their arguments:

> I hold that there is no such thing as a natural and unconquerable repugnance between varieties of men. All these artificial and arbitrary barriers give way before interest and enlightenment. . . . The hope of the world is in Human Brotherhood; in the union of mankind, not in exclusive nationalities.

Through their attempts to convince whites that blacks were their equals, the abolitionists played a conspicuous if not causal role in building a small but important constituency for emancipation and in undermining support for colonization.

Their work had not been easy, and men and women who had been in the crusade since the 1830's were weary. Garrison thought that the abolitionist movement was over with the ratification of the Thirteenth Amendment in 1865. He knew there was great work yet to be done—the work of educating, uplifting, and securing equal rights for the freedmen. But he thought that the antislavery societies should be disbanded and that former members should start new organizations or dedicate themselves as individuals to ending racism.

A good many abolitionists disagreed with Garrison. Stephen Foster, Frederick Douglass, Wendell Phillips, and Charles Remond, among others, thought that the fight against racism could go on through the old organizations. Douglass, recalling the earlier struggles for equal rights in New England, said, "That was good anti-slavery work twenty years ago; I do not see why it is not good anti-slavery work now."

Garrison withdrew from the American Anti-Slavery Society in 1865, taking a number of others with him. Garrison and his allies were subsequently active in the movement to aid the freedmen; they spoke out for civil rights and eventually for black suffrage. But again, as in the 1840's, Garrisonians generally failed to advocate the use of the more powerful economic and political weapons needed to supplement the work of moral suasion and charitable relief.

Even Wendell Phillips, who looked forward to using the American Anti-Slavery Society as a vehicle for a more radical, more thoroughgoing reconstruction of American society, failed to see the need for large-scale social planning. "I ask nothing more for the negro than I ask for the Irishman or German who comes to our shores," he said. Blacks "only ask this nation— 'Take your yoke off our necks.' "

The abolitionists, as James McPherson has demonstrated (1964), struggled long and hard in the post-emancipation period to achieve racial equality. But the abolitionists were weary; moreover, the individualism that was part of nineteenth-century radicalism persisted although their goal now required collective action and massive social engineering. And, as George Frederickson has shown (1965), the war had weaned some abolitionists away from idealism and "pointed them in the direction of a more conservative, 'realistic,' or practical approach to reform." Thus, aiding the freedmen never commanded the kind of loyalty and determination shown in the cause of the slave.

Nevertheless, the abolitionists did make some significant gains. They set up their own freedmen's aid movements, and as soon as it became clear that emancipation would result from the Civil War they began urging the government to adopt a uniform policy toward the freedmen.

Lewis Tappan was among the first to recognize the new opportunities and responsibilities for coping with sudden emancipation. Along with Simeon Jocelyn and George Whipple, thirty-year veterans of the antislavery crusade, Tappan directed the experimental work of the American Missionary Association on the cotton-rich Sea Islands off the coast of South Carolina. When Union forces had seized the sea islands of Port Royal Sound, the master class fled, leaving 10,000 black slaves who refused to run with them. The blacks remained to enjoy their sudden liberty, but soon found themselves without winter clothing or doctors, and the federal forces that occupied the islands often seized their provisions. Developments quickly reached crisis proportions. To meet this crisis, the Treasury Department, under Salmon P. Chase, the most radical member of Lincoln's original cabinet, helped to finance the organization of several private benevolent societies whose purpose was to send needed goods as well as ministers, doctors, teachers, and labor superintendents to the islands. The collective efforts of these freedmen's aid societies were known by late 1862 as "the Port Royal Experiment."

Many of the younger abolitionists who joined the Port Royal movement under the encouragement of J. Miller McKim hoped that the islands could be a model for the regeneration of American society, a model that included the education and rehabilitation of the slave and a conclusive demonstration of his capacity for freedom. Wendell Phillips and William Lloyd Garrison, however, were still unconvinced. Garrison declared that education of blacks is *"popular* work as compared with ours, and we may safely leave it to the support of the community at large, giving it all the incidental help in our power, but not making it our special work."

The Port Royal people made education and rehabilitation their special work. And they were successful. Blacks worked the government land for wages, and they needed no coercion; they showed extreme eagerness and ability to learn to read and write. The freedmen demonstrated beyond question, as Willie Lee Rose has shown (1964), a willing and able response to freedom. The true lesson of the experiment—that collective, intensive devotion to "building up" the freed black community paid off—was not well understood, however. For subsequent abolitionist and government efforts in the direction of massive social experimentation were generally few and short-lived.

Still, the pioneering work for freedmen's education throughout the country was supported primarily by abolitionists. Tappan, Jocelyn, and Whipple worked through the American Missionary Association. Henry I. Bowditch, who had converted to abolitionism in 1835 upon seeing Garrison mobbed, now supported the Boston Education Committee's work with freedmen. Other enthusiastic supporters of the new work among the abolitionists were John Greenleaf Whittier, Maria Weston Chapman, and Lydia Maria Child. Garrison, too, eventually came around.

Several thousand Northerners, most of them abolitionists, went South to instruct freedmen. Some devoted the rest of their lives to this work. Abolitionists were active in every aspect of the drive for the education of freedmen. They organized auxiliary societies, solicited funds, lectured, recruited teachers, wrote texts, and founded schools.

One instance of abolitionist work with Southern schools deserves attention as an example of what was possible. In February, 1865, Union troops marched into Charleston, South Carolina, accompanied by abolitionist James Redpath, a reporter for the New York *Tribune*. The Army seized all the school buildings and appointed Redpath superintendent of education. Within ten days, Redpath had hired teachers, obtained textbooks, and enrolled students. On March 4, the schools were formally opened to 1,200 freedmen and 300 white children. The Northern freedmen's aid societies supplied the money for salaries and books. By the end of March, more than 3,000 children of both races were in the schools. Most of the 83 teachers—25 of them black— were natives of Charleston. The students and the staff increased in numbers, and soon there were nine day schools and five night schools. Redpath returned North in June with praises for his work from the people of Charleston, Army officers, and abolitionists.

While abolitionists worked through local freedmen's aid societies, they kept up pressure for a government bureau. Some of them spent weeks in Washington lobbying for the Freedmen's Bureau Bill. When the Bureau was created in March, 1865, it became an important partner of the aid societies. The Bureau contributed school buildings and paid teachers' transportation costs. Ultimately the Bureau and the aid societies spent about $3,000,000 and gave 150,000 freedmen a rudimentary education.

The abolitionists who had pushed for a Freedmen's Bureau wanted more than government aid in their educational efforts. They wanted an agency "to make provision for the first necessities of the freedmen, to allot them lands out of those forfeited by the rebels [and] to organize and protect their labor." Abolitionist editor Edmund Quincy insisted in 1865, "If the monopoly of land be permitted to remain in the hands of the present rebel proprietors . . . the monopoly of labor might almost as well be given them, too." Wendell Phillips, Gerrit Smith, Lydia Maria Child, and others echoed these sentiments.

The promise of land for the freedmen was embodied in legislation creating the Freedmen's Bureau. About 50,000 former slaves did temporarily become landowners. Freedmen on South Carolina's Sea Islands had purchased several thousand acres of land with their wages, and freedmen from all over the southeastern United States were resettled with "possessory titles" on thousands of acres in South Carolina, Georgia, and Florida. President Andrew Johnson's amnesty program, however, which generally returned confiscated rebel estates, left the Bureau with very little land for this purpose. Some 4,000,000 freedmen continued to live on their former masters' acres. In most cases there was either resumption of exploitive paternalism or simply crass coercion. Moreover, most of the 50,000 freedmen who did become landowners, including those at Port Royal, ultimately were dispossessed by the amnesty program.

A majority of the Republican party including the Radicals remained opposed to further confiscation throughout the Reconstruction period. And several abolitionists, including Elizur Wright, Jr., continued to chide politicians who were willing to leave the land in the hands of the former slaveholders:

O ye mighty "practical" men! don't you know—are you not sensible —does it not enter your noodles to suspect—that if you have thirty thousand disloyal nabobs to own more than half the land of the South, they, and nobody else, will *be* the South? That they laugh, now in their sleeves, and by-and-bye will laugh out of their sleeves, at your schoolma'ams and ballot-boxes? *They who own the real estate of a country control its vote.*

The only thing the Freedmen's Bureau was able to accomplish in the way of economic aid was to oversee a contract labor system in the South. According to historian William McFeeley, the contracts drawn up by the Freedmen's Bureau were basically conservative. They often perpetuated slave work conditions, such as gang labor and corporal punishment. While the language of the contracts seemed to provide for payment of wages, this often did not occur. Even where wages were paid, there was an elaborate wage-docking system for "disciplinary" purposes. Sometimes freedmen made so little that at the end of a pay period they were forced to take loans from the planter, deepening their dependence.

Blacks had to try to improve their lot without outside help. In order to get better working conditions, they participated in deliberate work slowdowns. In their new contracts they demanded small "patches" of their own land, unsupervised work, and the right to care for their dependents. In return, the black farmer would give a percentage of his crop. The landowners reluctantly gave in to the freedmen's demands. But the freedmen were still to be disappointed with what amounted only to a sharecropping system. For the planters, after regaining political influence in the South, simply turned the new system to their advantage.

Land redistribution would not have solved all the freedmen's problems, but it certainly could have helped. The meager efforts in this area must be counted as one of the major failures of Reconstruction. Without land it was impossible for blacks in the South to become economically independent. And without economic independence the statutory citizenship and civil rights gained through abolitionists efforts were relatively worthless.

During the war and in the early years of Reconstruction, abolitionists and black citizens working throughout the country to establish racial justice made some minor gains: California, in 1863, repealed a law excluding black testimony against whites; Illinois, in 1865, repealed all its "black laws" except those relating to suffrage; in the same year, Massachusetts passed an omnibus act ending segregation in public accommodations; and Rhode Island and Connecticut passed laws ending separate schools; in 1866 the Indiana Supreme Court declared the state's worst "black laws" unconstitutional.

But otherwise progress was slow in these and other Northern states. And many Southern states, beginning with Mississippi in late 1865, began to enact "black codes" as a form of social control of the freedmen. This legislation was generally harsh and repressive and seemed almost to throw the black back into slavery. And yet in February, 1866, Johnson vetoed a bill empowering the Freedmen's Bureau to oversee the civil rights of blacks in the South.

The North, as we have seen, while not prepared to grant blacks the right to full participation in American society, did believe that the war had put a final end to slavery. When that decision seemed to be challenged by the supposedly vanquished slave power in the form of "black codes," and when Johnson's veto made it appear again, as in the 1850's, that the South had a stranglehold on the Presidency, abolitionists and Republicans in Congress were presented with an opportunity and a challenge to enlarge the area of the black's rights and privileges. For the North was again ready to act against Southern arrogance.

Congress, in April, 1866, passed a Civil Rights Act over President Johnson's veto, bestowing citizenship on blacks (legislation necessitated by the Dred Scott decision) and granting the same civil rights to all persons born in the United States except Indians. Abolitionists wished to include suffrage in those civil rights and put constant pressure on the Republican party to that end. In 1866, however, the North was not yet ready to give the suffrage to the black man. In fact, as late as 1868, only four states outside of New England and New York allowed blacks to vote. Colorado and Connecticut had rejected black suffrage in 1865; Ohio and Kansas did so in 1867; Missouri and Michigan, in 1868.

Race prejudice was so strong in the North that the issue of equal black suffrage constituted a clear threat to the Republicans. On the national level, they proceeded cautiously on the issue through 1868. But abolitionist pressure on this question apparently did convince and move some Republicans. Between 1865 and 1868 Republicans fought many battles in state legislatures and in state referenda in behalf of black suffrage. And in January, 1866, Republicans in Congress voted 116–15 for black suffrage in Washington, D.C.

In order to guarantee black suffrage throughout the country, abolitionists believed that a constitutional amendment was necessary. They hoped the amendment would ensure the black man citizenship and federal protection against state invasion of his civil rights, including the right to vote. In 1866 Congress hammered out a proposed Fourteenth Amendment, which the Southern states were expected to ratify as a condition of readmission to the Union. The proposed amendment was, despite abolitionist pressure, equivocal on racial questions and freedmen's rights —especially on suffrage. Instead of explicitly granting blacks the right to vote, it provided for proportionate reduction in representation if a state denied suffrage to male citizens of legal age.

The abolitionists were appalled. In a public letter Gerrit Smith asserted that if the South were readmitted to the Union under such a plan, she would gladly accept reduced representation in order to keep her black population disfranchised. Said Frederick Douglass, "To tell me that I am an equal American citizen, and in the same breath, tell me that my right to vote may be constitutionally taken from me by some other equal . . . citizens, is to tell me that my citizenship is but an empty name." Wendell Phillips accused Republicans who advocated such an amendment of being "occupied chiefly in keeping up their own organization. Let that party be broken that sacrifices principle to preserve its own existence."

Some modern historians agree with Phillips' charge that the Republicans were concerned primarily with the strength of their party. After all, they argue, the representation of the South, which was certain to be largely Democratic after Reconstruction, could be reduced under the Fourteenth Amendment; Republicans did campaign for the amendment in the North as a defense against Southern ascendancy. And some Republicans campaigned for the Fourteenth Amendment in the racist North as a protection for the white man. New York Senator Roscoe Conkling believed that if blacks were given "liberty and rights [in] the South, ... they will stay there and never come into a cold climate to die."

That Republican politicians used these arguments is no proof that they were cynical; it is simply an indication that they knew their audiences. There is no question that Republican politicians generally looked to strengthen their positions and the position of their party. But the voting behavior of Republican politicians between 1865 and 1868 seems to have been influenced by the abolitionists, for it was often enough in favor of equal rights to suggest that they saw the black man, and not their party, as the main beneficiary of the Fourteenth Amendment.

In any case, the abolitionists thought that the Fourteenth Amendment, finally ratified in 1868, was too weak. They favored an additional amendment explicitly prohibiting states from denying suffrage on the basis of race. Many of them wished as well to prohibit property requirements and literacy tests. As one abolitionist put it, forbidding only racial disfranchisement "will not prevent any state [from] adopting a property qualification, one of education, or any similar dodge." When the 1868 election was safely behind them, Republicans came forward with proposals for national action on black suffrage. The abolitionists' idea of prohibiting racial disfranchisement was accepted, but the proposed Fifteenth Amendment did not prohibit property requirements and literacy tests, and thereby allowed loopholes to the states.

Republican support of the Fifteenth Amendment was generally disadvantageous to the party. A Republican legislature that ratified the Fifteenth Amendment in New York, for example, was almost immediately swept out of office. Horace Greeley recognized that "the Negro question lies at the bottom of our [Republican] reverses ... thousands have turned against us because we purpose to enfranchise the Blacks. ... We have lost votes in the Free States by daring to be just to the Negro."

Nonetheless, the party, and especially its Radical wing, continued to fight for the Fifteenth Amendment. Abolitionists were heartened by their belief that they had succeeded in turning many Republicans away from expediency and toward real commitment to equal suffrage. By February, 1869, the Fifteenth Amendment was on its way to the states. Radical Republicans and abolitionists used a combination of persuasion and emotion in the North and political control in the South to bring about ratification of the amendment within thirteen months.

The American Anti-Slavery Society resolved at its annual convention in May, 1869, that the Fifteenth Amendment was the "capstone and completion of our movement; the fulfillment of our pledge to the Negro race; since it secures to them equal political rights with the white race, or, if any single right be still doubtful, places them in such circumstances that they can easily achieve it."

A few abolitionists urged that the Society remain in existence after ratification of the Fifteenth Amendment, to combat race prejudice, help the freedmen to obtain land, and agitate for strict enforcement of equal rights. Wendell Phillips, among the majority, disagreed, although he recognized the "continued obligation" of abolitionists "never to cease their individual and collateral work."

Most abolitionists remained individualistic, with an exaggerated confidence that the black man could now make his own way. Yet the society in which the freedman was expected to make his way had not been substantially changed from what it was during slavery. The numerically preponderant whites still feared blacks; and blacks, like others in the lower classes without economic independence, were still basically powerless.

The abolitionists' unwarranted confidence and individualistic perception moved them to end their history as an organized force in 1870. But the legal changes abolitionists had helped to effect proved inadequate. Discrimination continued in the wake of Civil War and Reconstruction, just as in the aftermath of the civil-rights victories of the 1950's, when blacks continued to be shortchanged in housing, employment, and education—even in Northern states with model civil-rights laws. In the South the virulently and violently antiblack Ku Klux Klan emerged after the war just as White Citizens Councils rose in that section after the civil-rights movement of the twentieth century.

And with the disappearance of the antislavery societies, the Republicans no longer had to face the collective strength of the abolitionists. Thus it was easy to accommodate themselves to the theories of racial inferiority so widely accepted in the North and South; and it was easy for them to succumb to the rationalization that national growth would by itself bring opportunity and rights to blacks. In short, it was easier for them, now that the abolitionists were not organized for watching so closely, to take the path of political expediency and abandon the black man.

In the late 1870's, abolitionists realized that much of what they had set out to do was not done. Lydia Maria Child believed that "the lamentable misfortune is that emancipation was not the result of a popular *moral sentiment,* but of a miserable 'military necessity.' It was not the 'fruit of righteousness,' and therefore it is not 'peace.'" She might have added—the lamentable misfortune is that for the abolitionists and for the North generally the cause of the freedman never commanded as much dedication as the cause of the slave.

Did the abolitionists fail, then? Since they sought a thorough reordering of American values and a restructuring of American society, one can say with much justification that they did. But to say the abolitionists failed is not to deprecate their long-range effect upon the course of events. The civil-rights crusade of the 1950's and 1960's and the current black-liberation movement owe a great debt to earlier black and white battlers for racial justice.

Furthermore, abolitionists did get Northerners to indict slavery, finally, as a threat to white men's liberty, and thus they fulfilled their aim of destroying a deeply rooted American institution. Those who argue that the costs were too high and that the violence of emancipation by its very nature prevented an enduring solution of the race problem have a point. But it may be that some problems will not be solved without violence, tragic and corrupting as violence is. Moreover, as we have seen, the vast majority of abolitionists wanted nothing to do with violence. They asked that the South be allowed to secede. But the North did not heed this advice.

What might have happened as a result of peaceful secession? Some historians argue that ultimately the South could not have withstood the powerful worldwide trend of industrialization and that, once industrial, the South would have freed the slaves voluntarily, to obtain a more efficient work force or for ideological considerations developing from the new material base. This theory, however, overlooks the appeal of slavery as a form of social control in places where blacks outnumbered whites. It also ignores the fact that blacks would have remained slaves for a much longer time if the North had not resisted secession.

Even if the South did eventually free the slaves in order to conform with a new bourgeois democratic ideology, there is no reason to believe that this peaceful emancipation would have ensured a more enduring solution to the race problem. After all, we have a significant prior example to serve as a model. Above the Mason-Dixon line, slavery had been abolished peacefully, and with little coercion. Yet, in the North, Negrophobia was, and to a significant degree still is, pervasive and active.

In any event, the North did not let the South go peacefully, despite the abolitionists. Once the war started, had the abolitionists not pushed for the end of slavery, its maintenance would probably have been guaranteed as part of the bargain of Reconstruction. Lincoln said as late as 1862:

My paramount objective in this struggle *is* to save the Union, and is *not* either to save or to destroy slavery. If I could save the Union without freeing *any* slave I would do it, and if I could save it by freeing *all* the slaves I would do it; and if I could save it by freeing some and leaving others alone I would also do that.

The President, early in the war, had proposed as a compromise a constitutional amendment *guaranteeing* that Congress would not interfere with slavery where it currently existed. Congress passed this amendment, and three Northern states had already ratified it in 1862.

It is true that the abolitionists seriously compromised their status as independent social critics by supporting the war, but in this way they helped to end slavery. It is legitimate to question the importance of this achievement in light of the position of blacks in modern America. But it is equally legitimate to suggest that slavery might still be with us if the abolitionists had not acted as they did in the 1860's. Had slavery become securely entrenched as a result of the war and thus truly a national institution, then America, in response to criticism, might have defensively twisted and tortured its political heritage until the ideals of democracy, as well as its reality, were killed.

Would the slaves themselves have risen up eventually in response to changes in the American economy, or later in harmony with "third-world" movements? Perhaps, but it is hard to conceive that such an uprising would long have remained non-violent. By the turn of the century, industrial America, with its ideology of freedom, was already becoming a counterrevolutionary force in the world. Surely it would have attempted to put down a rebellion within its own borders. And even had blacks achieved their freedom through rebellion, there is little reason to believe that they could at the same time have moved the society in the direction of racial justice.

The abolitionists did not succeed in implementing their revolutionary vision of a society based on brotherly love and racial equality. This may, after all, have been an impossible goal, but it probably required at least that the abolitionists maintain their role as agitators, continually propelling their fellow Americans toward higher levels of consciousness. In the 1830's and 1840's abolitionists acted toward this end. But after that time more and more of them admitted the existence of "limiting historical conditions" and turned to the "art of the possible." Ultimately, as we have seen, many abolitionists supported the Republican party and the Northern war effort, in the process increasingly compromising their humanitarian ideals.

The abolitionists' agitation over slavery, however, did initiate a cycle of events that led to the destruction of the "peculiar institution," if not of all its ramifications. Moreover, their work during and after the Civil War helped to enshrine in the Constitution the ideals of racial justice toward which this country still gropes its way. They were often short-sighted and sometimes insensitive, but they provided us with an example of men and women with the courage to risk painful self-examination, to measure the gap between reality and their aspirations for themselves and their society. Like some reformers today, black and white, they called for individual responsibility for the direction of society. Their plea was rejected; most people preferred to acquiesce in the drift of political and social events. This was the real failure. It would be more than a pity to repeat it.

Bibliographical Essay

General Sources

The best general survey of the abolitionist movement is Louis Filler's *The Crusade Against Slavery, 1830–1860* (New York: Harper & Row, 1960); serious students will further benefit by consulting Filler's excellent bibliography.

One should, where possible, read the abolitionists' own writings. For a bibliography of these, see Dwight Dumond's *Antislavery*, Part II (Ann Arbor: University of Michigan Press, 1961). The longer works of the abolitionists are increasingly available in reprints. Good anthologies of short pieces and excerpts with introductions and bibliographies are: John L. Thomas, *Slavery Attacked* (Englewood Cliffs, N.J.: Prentice-Hall, 1965); Louis Ruchames, *The Abolitionists* (New York: Capricorn, 1964); and Truman Nelson, *Documents of Upheaval: Selections from the Liberator* (New York: Hill & Wang, 1966). The best anthology of abolitionist literature is W. H. Pease and J. H. Pease, *The Antislavery Argument* (Indianapolis: Bobbs-Merrill, 1965).

Chapter 1

Historians are no longer content with the view that abolitionism was the expression of a psychologically disturbed class (David Donald, "Toward a Reconsideration of Abolitionists," in *Lincoln Reconsidered* [New York: Knopf, 1956]), or a way of releasing an exaggerated guilt (Stanley Elkins, *Slavery: A Problem in American Institutional and Intellectual Life* [Chicago: University of Chicago Press, 1959]. Aileen Kraditor, in *Means and Ends in American Abolitionism* (New York: Vintage Books, Random House, 1968), for example, recognized that the abolitionists had feelings of guilt but suggests that they had a realistic base for those feelings.

The anomaly of the most rigid institutionalized form of slavery existing within the most fluid, least institutionalized social structure had to make slavery seem morally wrong to those whites who took their Declaration of Independence seriously.

Martin Duberman, in *Charles Francis Adams* (Boston: Houghton Mifflin, 1961); in "Abolitionists and Psychology," *Journal of Negro History* 47 (July, 1962): 183–91; and in *James Russell Lowell* (Boston: Houghton Mifflin, 1966), has not only criticized the sociopsychological assumptions of the older image of the abolitionists; he has marshaled evidence that the crusaders were not generally neurotic in their motivation. And my own *New York Abolitionists: A Case Study of Political Radicalism* (Westport, Conn.: Greenwood, 1971), a systematic examination of available information on one hundred top abolitionist leaders, yielded a portrait of the radical reformer as a man who suffered no significant social frustration.

For the conservative origins of abolitionism, see Bertram Wyatt-Brown, "Prelude to Abolitionism," *Journal of American History* 58 (September, 1971): 316–41. For more on the historiography of abolitionism, see Martin L. Dillon, "The Abolitionists: A Decade of Historiography, 1959–1969," *Journal of Southern History* 35 (November, 1969): 506–22, and Bertram Wyatt-Brown, "Abolitionism: Its Meaning for Contemporary American Reform," *Midwest Quarterly* 8 (October, 1966): 41–55.

In *Antislavery Vanguard* (Princeton, N.J.: Princeton University Press, 1964), edited by Martin Duberman, there are several essays that review the historical literature on the abolitionist movement: Fawn Brodie, "Who Defends the Abolitionist?"; Larry Gara, "Who Was an Abolitionist?"; and Howard Zinn, "Abolitionists, Freedom-Riders, and the Tactics of Agitation." Another worthwhile essay is Betty Fladeland, "Who Were the Abolitionists?" in *Journal of Negro History* 43 (April, 1964): 99–115.

There are also several historiographical anthologies, the best of which are Richard O. Curry, ed., *The Abolitionists: Reformers or Fanatics?* (New York: Holt, Rinehart & Winston, 1965), and Hugh Hawkins, *The Abolitionists: Immediatism and the Question of Means* (Boston: D. C. Heath, 1964).

The significant literature on the dean of the abolitionists, William Lloyd Garrison, is ably reviewed in David A. Williams, "William Lloyd Garrison, the Historians, and the Abolitionist Movement," Essex Institute, *Historical Collections* 98 (April, 1962): 84–99, and Louis Filler, "Garrison Again, and Again: A Review Article," *Civil War History* 11 (March, 1965): 69–75.

Chapter 2

No one interested in the roots of abolitionism in early America can afford to neglect David Brion Davis's monumental study, *The Problem of Slavery in Western Culture* (Ithaca, N.Y.: Cornell University Press, 1966), which traces the intellectual history of antislavery from antiquity to the eve of the American Revolution, all the while building the provocative thesis that militant abolitionism was possible only after a series of significant changes in religious thinking. But also see Moses I. Finley, "The Idea of Slavery" *New York Review of Books* 3, No. 1: 7–10.

Winthrop Jordan's *White Over Black* (Chapel Hill: University of North Carolina Press, 1968) is a daring, brilliant work that will probably evoke dozens of new studies. Jordan contends, among other things, that the race prejudice of early white Americans (and indirectly of all Western whites) had such incredibly deep roots (perhaps even physiological roots) and was so irrational that attempts to counteract it through reasoned argument were severely handicapped. For a different view, see Louis Ruchames, "Sources of Racial Thought in Colonial America," *Journal of Negro History* 52 (October, 1963): 251–72.

A pioneering work on early abolitionism is Mary S. Locke's *Anti-Slavery in America, 1619–1808* (Boston: Ginn & Co., 1901). Less successful but filling an important gap is Alice Adams, *The Neglected Period of Anti-Slavery in America, 1808–1831* (Boston: Ginn & Co., 1908).

For the abolition of slavery in the Northern states, the student should read Arthur Zilversmit, *The First Emancipation* (Chicago: University of Chicago Press, 1967). Zilversmit makes a convincing case that the ideology of the American Revolution significantly aided the emancipation movement in the North. A similar theme is developed in Don B. Kates, "Abolition, Deportation, Integration: Attitudes Toward Slavery in the Early Republic," *Journal of Negro History* 53 (January, 1968): 33–47.

The religious motivation of the early abolitionists is the focus of Thomas Drake's *Quakers and Slavery in America* (New Haven: Yale University Press, 1950). The rise of early abolitionist sentiment is traced to a combination of religious benevolence and Revolutionary liberalism in Paul Boller, "Washington, the Quakers and Slavery," *Journal of Negro History* 46 (April, 1961): 83–88; and in D. S. Lovejoy, "Samuel Hopkins: Religion, Slavery and the Revolution," *New England Quarterly* 40 (June, 1967): 227–43.

For abolitionism in the South, a recent source is Gordon E. Finnie,

"The Antislavery Movement in the Upper South before 1840," *Journal of Southern History* 35 (August, 1969): 319–42. Other significant works in this area are Robert McColley, *Slavery and Jeffersonian Virginia* (Urbana: University of Illinois Press, 1964), and William Cohen, "Thomas Jefferson and the Problem of Slavery," *Journal of American History* 56 (December, 1969): 503–26.

Chapter 3

The theme of frustrated gradualism can be followed in Merton Dillon's fine biography of *Benjamin Lundy* (Urbana: University of Illinois Press, 1966). On the colonization movement, P. J. Staudenraus, *The African Colonization Movement* (New York: Columbia University Press, 1961) supersedes Early Lee Fox, *The American Colonization Society* (Baltimore: Johns Hopkins Press, 1919). For the relationship between religious revivalism and the rise of immediatism, the best essay is still David Brion Davis's "The Emergence of Immediatism in British and American Antislavery Thought," *Mississippi Valley Historical Review* 49 (September, 1962): 209–30. The student should also see in this regard Anne C. Loveland, "Evangelicalism and 'Immediate Emancipation' in American Antislavery Thought," *Journal of Southern History* 32 (May, 1966): 172–88; Timothy L. Smith, *Revivalism and Social Reform in Mid-Nineteenth Century America* (New York: Harper & Row, 1965); Whitney R. Cross, *Burned-Over District* (Ithaca, N.Y.: Cornell University Press, 1950); and Gilbert Hobbs Barnes, *The Anti-Slavery Impulse* (New York: Harcourt Brace & World, 1964).

The influence of British antislavery on American developments is explored in Frank Thistlethwaite, *The Anglo-American Connection in the Early Nineteenth Century* (Philadelphia: University of Pennsylvania Press, 1959); Thomas F. Harwood, "British Evangelical Abolitionism and American Churches in the 1830's," *Journal of Southern History* 28 (August, 1962): 287–306; Douglass H. Maynard, "The World's Anti-Slavery Convention of 1840," *Mississippi Valley Historical Review* 48 (December, 1960): 452–71; and C. Duncan Rice, "The Anti-Slavery Mission of George Thompson to the United States, 1834–1835," *Journal of American Studies* 2 (April, 1968): 13–31.

Chapter 4

Carleton Mabee's *Black Freedom* (New York: Macmillan, 1970) is the best work on the subject of moral suasion. The book is filled with exciting episodes of antislavery work as well as insightful analysis of the reformers themselves. Anyone interested in the possibilities of non-violence as a tool for change should be sure to peruse Mabee's masterful book.

Other useful sources are Lewis Perry, "Versions of Anarchism in the Antislavery Movement," *American Quarterly* 20 (Winter, 1968): 769–82; and Louis Filler, "Nonviolence and Abolitionism," *University Review* 30 (Spring, 1964): 172–78.

The greatest of the moral-suasion abolitionists was William Lloyd Garrison. To date there is no completely satisfactory biography of this leader. The best of the most recent works is Walter Merrill, *Against Wind and Tide* (Cambridge: Harvard University Press, 1963). John L. Thomas, *The Liberator* (Boston: Little, Brown, 1963) is marred by the author's hostility toward Garrison. It is possible for the enterprising student to develop his own portrait by reading Garrison's newspaper, *The Liberator* (which is on microfilm in many college libraries), or Truman Nelson's *Document of Upheaval: Selections from the Liberator* (New York: Hill & Wang, 1966) and *The Letters of William Lloyd Garrison*, edited by Walter Merrill and Louis Ruchames (Cambridge: Harvard University Press, 1971). One should also see Aileen Kraditor's excellent *Means and Ends in American Abolitionism* (New York: Vintage Books, Random House, 1968); James B. Stewart, "The Aims and Impact of Garrisonian Abolitionism, 1840–1860," *Civil War History* 15 (September, 1969): 197–209; and Bertram Wyatt-Brown, "William Lloyd Garrison and Antislavery Unity: A Reappraisal," *Civil War History* 13 (March, 1967): 5–24.

On other leaders in the moral-suasion movement, see Gerda Lerner, *The Grimké Sisters from South Carolina* (Boston: Houghton Mifflin, 1967); Milton Meltzer, *Tongue of Flame: The Life of Lydia Maria Child* (New York: T. Y. Crowell, 1965); Irving H. Bartlett, *Wendell Phillips: Brahmin Radical* (Boston: Beacon Press, 1961); and Bertram Wyatt-Brown's fine book *Lewis Tappan and the Evangelical War Against Slavery* (Cleveland: Case Western Reserve, 1969). A useful book not directly concerned with abolitionism but dealing with many moral-suasion abolitionists and the implications of their ideology is Peter Brock, *Radical Pacifists in Antebellum America* (Princeton, N.J.: Princeton University Press, 1968).

George Frederickson's *The Black Image in the White Mind: The Debate on Afro-American Character and Destiny, 1817–1914* (New York: Harper & Row, 1971) is an excellent place to begin to try to understand the roots of the race prejudice abolitionists were up against in Jacksonian America.

Chapter 5

The political abolitionists are sorely neglected. The only book dealing primarily and directly with the Liberty party is Theodore C. Smith, *The Liberty and Free Soil Parties in the North West* (Cambridge: Harvard University Press, 1897). Aileen Kraditor's *Means and Ends in American Abolitionism* is very helpful, but a definitive history of the Liberty party remains to be written.

Biographical studies have been written on a number of the political abolitionists: Betty Fladeland, *James G. Birney* (Ithaca, N.Y.: Cornell University Press, 1955), is sympathetic and scholarly; Ralph Harlow, *Gerrit Smith* (Syracuse: Syracuse University Press, 1939), is well researched but exceedingly hostile; Bertram Wyatt-Brown, *Lewis Tappan* (Cleveland: Case Western Reserve, 1969), combines an incisive study of the reformer's life with a penetrating analysis of nineteenth-century America. For a study of the motivation of some of the political abolitionists, see Gerald Sorin, *New York Abolitionists* (Westport, Conn.: Greenwood, 1971).

On the general question of violence in the movement, one should consult Carleton Mabee, *Black Freedom* (New York: Macmillan, 1970). Mabee contends that violence by abolitionists or slaves was almost always counterproductive, leading in most cases to greater repression. He speculates that the broad application of nonviolent principles by abolitionists, in the manner of the followers of Martin Luther King, and the broad use of nonviolent mass action to change white minds might very well have ended slavery without a civil war.

Bertram Wyatt-Brown wrote in "Abolitionism: Its Meaning for Contemporary American Reform," *Midwest Quarterly* 8 (October, 1966): 41–55, that most abolitionists fortunately recognized that overtly violent means would probably have shocked the nation into an era of tyrannical repression. But once the war came in 1861, it was necessary, he contends, for the abolitionists to direct it against slavery. Otherwise, the Union would have been restored with the "peculiar institution" more firmly entrenched.

Stanley Elkins, in *Slavery: A Problem in American Intellectual and Institutional Life* (Chicago: University of Chicago Press, 1959), thinks that slavery could have been abolished without violence if the abolitionists had worked to ameliorate the evils of the institution instead of attacking it as "a problem in pure morality." Elkins maintains that the abolitionists were alienated from the sources of power and were against using institutions (such as politics and the church) as weapons in their crusade. This, according to Elkins, prevented abolitionists from proposing specific laws—for example, to protect the sanctity of the slave family, to mitigate cruelty to slaves, and otherwise to recognize the slave's humanity.

Another important article in this area is John Demos, "The Anti-Slavery Movement and the Problem of Violent Means," *New England Quarterly* 37 (December, 1964): 501–26. And on the specific violence of John Brown see Louis Ruchames's sympathetic *John Brown Reader* (New York: Abelard-Schuman, 1959) and Stephen B. Oates's critical *To Purge This Land with Blood* (New York: Harper & Row, 1970).

Chapter 6

The Negroes in the movement have finally been given extended treatment in Benjamin Quarles's fine book *Black Abolitionists* (New York: Oxford University Press, 1969). Reading the earlier work of Charles H. Wesley is still very worthwhile. See especially "The Participation of Negroes in Anti-Slavery Political Parties," *Journal of Negro History* 39 (January, 1944): 32–74; "The Negro in the Organization of Abolition," *Phylon* 2 (1941): 223–35; and "The Negroes of New York in the Emancipation Movement," *Journal of Negro History* 24 (January, 1939): 65–103.

On relations between black and white abolitionists, see Leon Litwack, "Abolitionist Dilemma: The Anti-Slavery Movement and the Northern Negro," *New England Quarterly* 34 (March, 1961): 50–73; "The Emancipation of the Negro Abolitionist," in Duberman, ed., *Antislavery Vanguard* (Princeton, N.J.: Princeton University Press, 1965); and Larry Gara, "The Professional Fugitive in the Abolitionist Movement," *Wisconsin Magazine of History*, Spring, 1965, pp. 196–204.

For specific material on black militancy, students should consult Howard H. Bell, "Expressions of Negro Militancy in the North, 1840–1860," *Journal of Negro History* 42 (October, 1957): 247–61. For a more recent interpretation of Negro militancy with constructive presentist overtones, see Jane and William Pease, "Black Power—the Debate in 1840," *Phylon* 29 (September, 1968): 19–26. For the South's reaction to black militancy, see Clement Eaton, "A Dangerous Pamphlet in the Old South," *Journal of Southern History* 2 (1936): 323–34, and William Freehling, *Prelude to Civil War* (New York: Harper & Row, 1965).

The indexes of the *Journal of Negro History* and *Negro History Bulletin* list numerous articles on individual black leaders. While these articles are uneven in quality, all contain useful information.

Frederick Douglass's own work has been widely reprinted in many editions. See especially *My Bondage and My Freedom* (New York: Johnson Publishing Co., 1968), and Philip Foner, ed., *Life and Writings of Frederick Douglass* (New York: International Publishers, 1950–55). Benjamin Quarles has written a solid biography, *Frederick Douglass* (Washington, D.C.: Associated Publishers, 1948). For an excellent brief analysis of Douglass's reform career, see August Meier, "Frederick Douglass' Vision for America: A Case Study in Nineteenth-Century Negro Protest," in Harold Hyman, ed., *Freedom and Reform* (New York: Harper & Row, 1967).

The writings of black abolitionist leaders are increasingly available in reprint edition. Invaluable is Carter G. Woodson, *The Mind of the Negro as Reflected in Letters Written During the Crisis, 1800–1860* (New York: Russell & Russell, 1969). There are various editions of the autobiographies of Samuel Ringgold Ward, William Wells Brown, and other black abolitionists. These are well worth consulting, but unfortunately most reprints are not well edited.

An excellent picture of the free Negro in the Northern states is presented in Leon Litwack, *North of Slavery* (Chicago: University of Chicago Press, 1961). John Hope Franklin, *From Slavery to Freedom* (New York: Knopf, 1967), is also useful on this subject.

Chapter 7

The South's reaction to the abolitionist crusade is perceptively and imaginatively dealt with by Charles Sellers's "The Travail of Slavery," in *Southerner as American* (Chapel Hill: University of North Carolina Press, 1960), and William Freehling, *Prelude to Civil War* (New York: Harper & Row, 1965), especially chapters 3 and 5. For the provocative thesis that the South was a precapitalist society, see Eugene Genovese, *The Political Economy of Slavery* (New York: Vintage, 1967), and *The World the Slaveholders Made* (New York: Vintage, 1971). Still useful is W. S. Jenkins, *Pro-Slavery Thought in the Old South* (Chapel Hill: University of North Carolina Press, 1935). For more recent views, see Ralph E. Morrow, "The Proslavery Argument Revisited," *Mississippi Valley Historical Review* 48 (June, 1961): 70–94, and David Donald, "Proslavery Argument Reconsidered," *Journal of Southern History* 37 (February, 1971): 3–18.

For the early Northern reaction, see Lorman Ratner, *Powder Keg: Northern Opposition to the Antislavery Movement, 1831–1840* (New York: Basic Books, 1968); Leonard Richard's excellent *Gentlemen of Property and Standing: Anti-Abolitionist Mobs in Jacksonian America* (New York: Oxford University Press, 1970); and Linda K. Kerber, "Abolitionists and Amalgamators: The New York City Race Riots of 1834," *New York History* 48 (January, 1967): 28–40.

On the significant relationship between the violation of civil liberties and the growth of antislavery, Russel B. Nye's *Fettered Freedom* (East Lansing: Michigan State University Press, 1949) is indispensable. See also Bertram Wyatt-Brown, "Abolitionists and the Postal Campaign of 1835," *Journal of Negro History* 50 (October, 1965): 227–38; James McPherson, "Fight Against the Gag Rule: Joshua Leavitt and Anti-Slavery Insurgency in the Whig Party, 1839–1842," *Journal of Negro History* 48 (July, 1963): 177–95; Samuel Flagg Bemis, *John Quincy Adams and the Union* (New York: Knopf, 1956); and Silvan Tomkins, "The Psychology of Commitment: The Constructive Role of Violence and Suffering for the Individual and for His Society," in Martin Duberman, ed., *Antislavery Vanguard*, (Princeton, N.J.: Princeton University Press, 1964).

On the development of antislavery politics (Free Soil, Republican) as distinct from abolitionist politics (Liberty party), see Larry Gara, "Slavery and the Slave Power: A Crucial Distinction," *Civil War History* 15 (March, 1969): 5–18; Richard Sewell, *John P. Hale and the Politics of Abolition* (Cambridge: Harvard University Press, 1965); James B. Stewart, *Joshua Giddings and the Tactics of Radical Politics, 1795–1864* (Cleveland: Case Western Reserve, 1969); Chaplain W. Morrison, *Democratic Politics and Sectionalism: The Wilmot Proviso Controversy* (Chapel Hill: University of North Carolina Press, 1967); Martin Duberman, "Northern Response to the Antislavery Movement," in his *Antislavery Vanguard*; Dwight L. Dumond, *Anti-Slavery Origins of the Civil War in the United States* (Ann Arbor: University of Michigan Press, 1939), and four works by Eric Foner: "Politics and Prejudice: The Free Soil Party and the Negro, 1849–1852," *Journal of Negro History* 50 (October, 1965); "Racial Attitudes of New York Free Soilers," *New York History* 46 (October, 1965): 311–29; "Wilmot Proviso Revisited," *Journal of American History* 56 (September, 1969): 62–79; *Free Soil, Free Labor, Free Men: The Ideology of the Republican Party Before the Civil War* (New York: Oxford University Press, 1970).

Several recent books emphasize the racist dimension of antislavery sentiment, notably Eugene H. Berwanger, *The Frontier Against Slavery* (Urbana: University of Illinois Press, 1967), and V. Jacques Voegeli, *Free but Not Equal* (Chicago: University of Chicago Press, 1967). For a balanced view, the student should also consult W. R. Brock, *An American Crisis* (London: St. Martin's Press, 1963); Lawanda and John Cox, "Negro Suffrage and Republican Politics," *Journal of Southern History* 33 (August, 1967): 303–30; and Glenn M. Linden, "A Note on Negro Suffrage and Republican Politics," *Journal of Southern History* 36 (August, 1970): 411–20.

Chapter 8

The abolitionists are often viewed as failures, even by sympathetic historians, because they never fulfilled their central aim of changing white America's negative consciousness about blacks. On this see Merton Dillon, "The Failure of the American Abolitionists," *Journal of Southern History* 25 (May, 1959):159–77. Willie Lee Rose, *Rehearsal for Reconstruction* (New York: Vintage, 1964), contends that the abolitionists failed because they were too individualistic and anti-institutional. Patrick Riddleberger, "The Radicals' Abandonment of the Negro During Reconstruction," *Journal of Negro History* 45 (April, 1960): 88–102, and Leon Litwack, *North of Slavery* (Chicago: University of Chicago Press, 1961), suggest that white abolitionist racism, conscious or otherwise, played a part in the failure.

On the other hand, James McPherson, in *Struggle for Equality* (Princeton, N.J.: Princeton University Press, 1964), wrote that abolitionists did not abandon their moral fervor after the Civil War began but instead fought valiantly for equal rights for the freedmen. Failure was primarily due to hesitant or recalcitrant Northern politicians. McPherson contends that there were advances toward racial justice, and that these were in part the result of abolitionist activity.

For recent views that are less confident about the durability of abolitionist victory, see C. Vann Woodward, "Seeds of Failure: The Radical Race Policy," in Harold Hyman, ed., *New Frontiers of Reconstruction* (Urbana: University of Illinois Press, 1966); Merton Dillon, "Abolitionists as a Dissenting Minority," in Alfred F. Young, ed., *Dissent* (DeKalb: Northern Illinois University Press, 1968), and Carleton Mabee, *Black Freedom* (New York: Macmillan, 1970). A challenging article in regard to the fruits of war is John S. Rosenberg, "Toward a New Civil War Revisionism," *American Scholar* 38 (Spring, 1969): 250–73.

For a general historiographical approach to this period, see Richard O. Curry, "Abolitionists and Reconstruction: A Critical Appraisal," *Journal of Southern History* 34 (November, 1968): 527–45.

Index